BETTER INTERNAL COMMUNICATION

How to add value, be more strategic and fast-track your career

LESLEY ALLMAN

R^ethink

*To Jim, Margaret, John and Lynda, my parents
and in-laws – you inspire me*

*To Andrew, my husband – you complete me
(and you had me at hello)*

*To William and Elisabeth, my son and daughter –
you make me so proud*

Contents

Foreword

Communication professionals are in an incredibly visible role inside organisations. Everything you write and advise is up for scrutiny and you're turned to as a trusted advisor. It's an invigorating, fascinating and vibrant role. It can also be frustrating, isolating and challenging.

I've spent two decades working in the field of communications and, despite new approaches and channels entering the profession, the fundamental principles of good, effective internal communication remain unchanged. When you work intentionally as an internal communicator, you need to seek evidence to reinforce your instinct, craft meaningful stories from data and demonstrate your influencing prowess. The onus is on comms pros to invest in their own professional development, and I know you'll find this book a valuable read. It contains ideas and actions you can immediately apply to your work. If you are looking to become a strategic internal communication professional and want to know how to be recognised as one, you're in the right place.

I welcome this book and I'm encouraged by Lesley's focus on supporting internal communicators through its publication. Lesley invited me to speak at the Institute of Internal Communication's Central Region conference back in 2013, when she was Director of the Central Region. She has extensive experience at a senior level, and I admire her thoughtful approach to internal communication. Lesley guides you through this book, explaining her ABCDE model and teaching you how to increase your knowledge, packing in practical examples to bring the thinking to life. Her intention is to help internal communicators enhance their careers, and the model provides a logical set of questions for you to go through. I know Lesley has designed the five steps so that you'll be well on the way to creating a professional and effective communication plan.

As a result of working through the ABCDE model, you will have what you need to know to put an effective, strategic communication plan in place. I urge you to keep focused on business outcomes as you read through it, take time to reflect on what she shares and think about how it applies to your own organisation.

Knowing how visible internal communicators are, I hope this book encourages and inspires you to take great strides in your career. Keep it to hand, as you'll want to refer to it time and time again.

Rachel Miller CHART PR FCIPR PGDIP FIIC
Founder, All Things IC
www.allthingsic.com

Introduction

L et's face it – everyone thinks they're an expert in internal communication.

In other professions, everyone else in the room respects the fact that the experts are trained and experienced in their field. When an accountant or lawyer is talking, it is assumed that they know best. But when it comes to communication, everyone from the CEO to their PA has an opinion.

As a communication professional, the onus is on you to raise your game which, in turn, will enable you to fast-track your career. To do that, you will need to develop and demonstrate your expertise. You must be able to show that what you are recommending and doing is based on real knowledge and experience that others simply don't have.

In over two decades as an internal communication specialist, I've learnt not only the best ways to devise and deliver effective internal communication, but also how to be recognised as the expert – a trusted advisor. I've spent my career learning and applying the craft of communications as a consultant, in-house and as an independent practitioner, working on internationally recognised brands. My experience has given me a unique insight into what works and what doesn't in terms of raising your game and fast-tracking your career.

Raising your game

Sometimes the focus is too much on just getting stuff out there, ie on the content and channels of communication. Of course, these are important, but communication is only effective when it has actually landed – when it has been received, digested, understood and acted on. Crafting some beautiful words and sending them out, even if this is done using the latest must-have channels, doesn't guarantee your message is communicated. There is a difference between informing people and engaging them. Internal communication can achieve both, but only if it's done properly.

To help organisations to think and act more strategically when it comes to internal communication, I've developed and applied a number of tried-and-tested techniques and models.

These include the ABCDE model, which ensures the right level of priority and focus is given to each of the five vital steps in any communication strategy: Audiences, Behaviours, Content, Delivery and Evaluation. This framework can be applied to communication challenges large and small, and I will share it with you in this book.

And it's not all about big budgets – you can produce great results without money for shiny new channels or campaigns and without extra resources to grow the communications team or increase the output. The advice in this book will help you to use the resources you have more effectively, to concentrate on what adds value and to identify – and stop doing – the things that are a waste of time and money.

Fast-tracking your career

To get on in your communications career, you need to be seen as more than just a postbox-person whose primary role is sending stuff out to employees. You need to show you know how to devise and deliver strategic internal communication that adds value for your organisation and its employees.

To be heard as a respected voice at the top table, you must prove your worth by demonstrating that, as a communication professional, you:

- Understand the commercials and the strategy of the organisation

- Can contribute to high-level conversations, using the sort of data and evidence that your top team recognises and respects

- Are creative and practical enough to come up with impactful and workable solutions to engage employees

- Can effectively mobilise employees to do whatever the business needs from them to successfully deliver the strategy

I've been doing this successfully for more than twenty years and now I'm sharing all my most useful learnings. I will set out approaches and actions that you can immediately apply to step up what you do and how you are perceived. This book contains everything you need to know to become and be recognised as a strategic internal communication professional. It will enable you to step up your knowledge, thinking and delivery, to increase your effectiveness and impact, and, ultimately, to enhance your career.

Everyone *thinks* they're an expert in internal communication. After reading this book, you'll be able to demonstrate that you *are* one.

Key

Throughout the book there are sections that will help you to focus on learnings and key takeaways:

 Exercises – questions and techniques to practise putting ideas into action

 Models – easy to follow steps and processes to inform your planning and delivery

 Tips and ideas – tried-and-tested recommendations to apply anytime

 Musings – some of my own stories and experiences, mostly about music, to inspire you (as the musician Duane Allman – no relation – said, 'There's a lot of different forms of communication, but music is absolutely the purest one, man.')

PART ONE
ADD VALUE

As you are reading this, it's safe to assume you understand and believe in the value of internal communication. However, that is not the case for everyone. I've met the following:

The few who just naturally get it – if that is the case in your organisation, then you're very lucky. You can skip Chapter 1 and move on.

The few who will *never* get it – if you think that applies to your top team, then you're unlikely to be able to change them, and you're even less likely to be getting the sort of experience that will add value to your career, so you may want to consider moving on. In which case, Parts Two and Three of this book will be particularly useful.

The majority who will get it if you can convince them that effective communication will support the commercial goals of the business – if that's the case in your organisation, then read on: Chapter 1 is for you.

1

The Value Of Internal Communication

Internal communication is sometimes considered a 'soft' subject – something that is a nice-to-have rather than a must-have in organisations. This couldn't be further from the truth. Anyone who thinks internal communication is only about telling employees stuff so they feel a bit better informed, or happier, is missing the point.

Internal communication is about ensuring that employees know what they need to do to deliver the company strategy. In that respect it is a 'hard' subject that can add as much value as any other professional function, such as finance, marketing or HR.

According to the Chartered Institute of Personnel and Development (CIPD), 'Effective internal communication

is important for developing **trust** within an organisation and has a significant impact on **employee engagement, organisational culture** and, ultimately, **productivity.'**
(December 2020, my emphasis.)

Let's look at each of these highlighted terms in turn,
considering the communicator's role and how it adds
value.

Trust

The Edelman Trust Barometer is a global survey which
measures the average percentage of trust in NGOs,
business, government and media. In 2021, for the first
time in its twenty-one-year history, it found business
to be the only trusted institution.

Of 33,000 people surveyed, 61% said that communication from their employer was their most trusted source
of information, higher than communication from national government (58%), traditional media (57%) and
social media (39%). As trust in external institutions
falls, respondents place even higher reliance on 'my
employer' at 76%, and 'my employer CEO' at 63%.

In addition, business was the only institution considered to be both ethical and competent, outscoring
government by forty-eight points on competency and
scoring almost as highly as NGOs on ethics.

These findings certainly put an increased responsibility on leaders to live up to the trust that has been placed in them and to do the right thing by their employees. In fact, the report found that the top trust-building action for business is now guarding information quality and ensuring that reliable, trustworthy information goes out to their employees.

The role of internal communicators in providing employees with the right communication content, channels, and capability has never been more important.

Employee engagement

It seems obvious that if you communicate effectively with your employees, they are much more likely to be engaged with your organisation, to have a more positive attitude towards their work and to be willing to go the extra mile. The work of organisations like Engage for Success, a voluntary movement promoting employee engagement, enables us to be even more precise about exactly what the value of this is and what is required to attain it.

Engage for Success promotes employee engagement as 'a better way to work that benefits individual employees, teams, and whole organisations'. The movement, which recently formed an alliance with CIPD, grew out of a report to government published over a decade ago, which identified the benefits of employee engagement and the four key enablers. The report was called *Engaging for Success*, although it's more commonly known as the *MacLeod Report*, and I was one of the original contributors.

David MacLeod and Nita Clarke researched published academic work and interviewed a wide range of practitioners for the *Engaging for Success* study. They found that although there is no one-size-fits-all approach to successful employee engagement, there are four common themes that are frequently cited as critical enablers.

These themes, over which internal communicators have considerable control and influence, are listed below. They have been reviewed and updated since their original publication and continue to be useful tools with which organisations can analyse the effectiveness of their internal communication and engagement activities.

Engage for Success – the Four Enablers

1. **Strategic narrative:** A clearly expressed story delivered by prominent leadership about the purpose of the organisation, why it has the vision it has and how individuals contribute to that purpose. Employees have a clear line of sight between their job and the narrative and understand where their work fits in.

2. **Engaging managers:** Engaging managers facilitate and empower their teams rather than restrict or control their staff. They are people-focused, treating individuals with appreciation and respect, and helping them to develop and grow their capabilities.

3. **Employee voice:** Employees are asked for their thoughts, are listened to and see that their opinions count and make a difference. Employees are key to problem-solving and are encouraged to contribute what they think, know and can do to solve organisational problems.

4. **Organisational integrity:** The organisation's values are evident in day-to-day practice. Leaders and managers are walking the talk. There is no gap between what they say and what they do.

 Traffic Light Exercise

Take a look at the descriptions of Engage for Success's Four Enablers and score your organisation on each of them as follows:

Green: I see this demonstrated often or all the time.

Amber: I see this demonstrated some of the time.

Red: I see this demonstrated rarely or never.

Consider your responses and what you can do to improve them.

In a subsequent report, *The Evidence*, published in 2012, Engage for Success demonstrated that companies with top quartile engagement scores demonstrated:

- Twice the annual net profit
- 2.5 times greater revenue growth
- 12% higher customer advocacy
- 40% lower employee turnover

What's more, the same report showed that while companies with high engagement scores have been shown to enjoy positive benefits, those with low engagement scores are disadvantaged in areas such as:

- **Health and Safety,** with 62% more accidents
- **Innovation,** with 3% creativity reported in employees with low engagement versus 56% in highly engaged employees

Organisational culture

There are lots of definitions of organisational culture. In their 1982 book *Corporate Cultures*, Deal and Kennedy contend that it simply comes down to 'how we do things around here', while a 2018 Gallup report says that 'culture is the optimal performance driver'. This is true in that it empowers employees, giving them freedom within a framework, so they can get on with delivering high-level goals knowing that they're doing the right thing, ie acting in line with the company culture. To do this effectively, however, employees have to be clear about exactly what the desired culture is. If they're not, there's a danger that everyone has their own interpretation and does their own thing, which could result in some undermining the desired culture rather than supporting it.

Communicators have an important role to play in defining and communicating organisational culture. This applies not just at the implementation of a new culture but as an ongoing reinforcement, celebrating the right behaviours and reminding employees of what is expected of them. This is another way that you add value to your organisation, and once again it is something that can be measured in bottom-line benefits.

Gallup's research shows a direct link between employees' understanding of their organisational culture and measures of business health. They found that among US employees, four out of ten strongly agree with the statement, 'The mission or purpose of my company makes me feel my job is important'. By moving that score to eight out of ten employees, organisations could see a 41% reduction in absenteeism, a 50% drop in safety incidents and a 33% improvement in quality. These also represent areas where major cost savings can be made – and measured.

Productivity

Another key measure identified by Engage for Success in their *The Evidence* report is that organisations in the top quartile of employee engagement had 18% higher productivity than those in the bottom quartile. A McKinsey & Company report also found that employee productivity increases by 20 to 25% in organisations where employees are connected.

According to the Corporate Leadership Council, increased productivity is the result of employees understanding the connection between their job and the overall business strategy. In fact, this alone can improve performance by 12%.

 ## Make regular deposits into the Bank of Communication

With a recent Chinese takeaway, I got a mysterious envelope with the words 'Bank of Communication' on it. Rather disappointingly, all it held was a voucher promising free fortune cookies with my next order. But it reminded me about the importance of making regular deposits into the Bank of Communication. Like any bank account, the more you put into it – via ongoing, effective internal communication – the more you will have to call on when times get tough.

As we saw in 2020, those organisations that had built up a positive balance in their internal communication accounts before the coronavirus pandemic hit were able to draw on those reserves when times got tough.

The lesson is simple: don't wait for a crisis to communicate with your employees, make a habit of it. You will be repaid with ongoing trust and engagement – which are even better than free fortune cookies!

Summary

Despite all of this evidence of the value that internal communication can bring to organisations, many of you still aren't confident that your leaders or colleagues understand your role, or the value you add.

Parts Two and Three of this book will help you address this.

Musing 1
Glastonbury: Have I Told You Lately

The first time I went to Glastonbury Festival was 1989. Tickets were £28 and the headliners were Van Morrison, Elvis Costello and Suzanne Vega.

I arranged to meet my boyfriend there. Even then, the capacity was 65,000 and of course there were no mobile phones, so we had to rely on notes. On arrival at the meeting point it soon became clear that, even if a note had been left, we'd never find it among the hundreds of scribbled bits of paper – many now trampled in the mud.

There was some urgency as I'd arrived straight from work and my boyfriend not only had our tent, but also my festival clothing. As darkness fell, we realised we'd never find them, so we'd better pitch my friend's tent, sleep the night there, then resume our search the next morning.

Eventually we found a suitable site to squeeze the tent into, and were about to get into it when we heard familiar voices. My boyfriend and his mate were staggering past and, it turned out, of all the tents, in all the fields, they were in the tent next door to us!

Internal communicators note – don't rely on the famous Glastonbury ley lines to work their magic. When making a plan, make sure it's clear, workable and well understood by all parties.

And as for that boyfriend? Reader, I married him.

PART TWO
BE STRATEGIC

'The answer is a newsletter/intranet/video/ESN/ app [delete as applicable].'

Now, what was the question?

Over the years as an internal communicator, there have been various shiny new communication solutions that seem like they will deliver all the answers, no matter what the question. Communicators, their bosses and clients tend to gravitate towards these things as if they are a silver bullet that will solve all of their communication problems.

I've often been briefed by a senior leader or a client to deliver a newsletter/intranet/video/ESN/app, or whatever the latest in-thing is, and although it would be easy to do exactly what they ask, if you aspire to be a trusted advisor and to add real value, then my advice is not to take their request at face value. Always dig a bit deeper. Find out what their real question is – then you have a good chance of coming up with the right answer.

Remember, you are the internal communication expert, not them. Demonstrate this by working with them and taking a strategic and professional approach to their request so that you can help them to identify the solution(s) that will really work, rather than simply applying a quick fix.

The good news is that there is a simple, tried-and-tested model that you can apply to achieve this. It is easy for anyone to understand and believe in, and it will ensure you deliver the right communication solution every time. You can apply it to everything from a simple announcement to a major change programme. It is something I've been developing and refining during my career, and it's a game changer. It's as simple as ABCDE.

 ## The ABCDE model of internal communication©

This model provides a logical set of questions for you to find out everything you need to know to put an effective strategic communication plan in place. It will prevent you, your clients, and in-house contacts from leaping straight to an obvious solution (usually a channel) that may or may not deliver what is really needed. Simply follow these five steps and you'll be well on the way to creating a professional and effective internal communication plan that will not only deliver what is needed from a business outcome point of view, but will also make you – and them – look great.

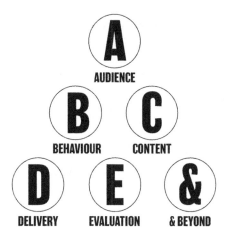

Audience

- Who is your communication aimed at?

- Who are you trying to reach?

- Who are your potential enablers and blockers?

Behaviour

- Why are you communicating with them? What is the objective?

- What do we want people to do, say, think and feel?

- How can you motivate them to make the required change?

Content

- What key messages do you want to convey?

- Will your content connect? Is it clear, compelling, in context and concise?

- Is your role to create, co-create or curate the content?

Delivery

- What channels should you choose? Verbal, online or print?

- Do you need to build your line managers' or leaders' communication capability?

- Do you have enough two-way channels? Are you really listening?

Evaluation

- What does success look like? How will you know if your communication has achieved its objectives?

- What measures do you need? Before and after? Inputs or outputs? Qualitative or quantitative?

- What next? How will you demonstrate that you've listened to and acted on the results?

The rest of Part Two is devoted to digging a bit deeper into each of these five steps (and a few other areas that don't fit neatly into the model), sharing the approaches and the latest thinking about each, so that you will have the knowledge and the confidence to push back on those glib requests for a newsletter/intranet/video/ESN/app and become instead the go-to person for truly strategic solutions.

2
Audience

The first step to effective communication is understanding your audience. The very first questions internal communicators must always ask are:

- Who is your communication aimed at?

- Who are you trying to reach?

- Who are your potential enablers and blockers?

Getting to know your audience is critical. And your audience is not just those you have direct contact with, but also – in fact, especially – those who are more remote and harder to reach.

To avoid the cookie-cutter approach, you must put yourself in the employees' shoes, so you can tailor your communication to them. Ideally you should make each employee feel like the communication they receive is directly relevant to them. In digital marketing, they call this 'mass personalisation' – it's the opposite of 'one size fits all'. You can only do this properly if you really know and understand your audience.

While this exercise is primarily about identifying those who will be on the receiving end of your communication, you must not forget the stakeholders who are not necessarily audiences for your communication, but are crucial to your effective work as a communicator. These are:

- Your potential **enablers,** ie those who can provide valuable input to help you shape, deliver and sustain your communication

- Your potential **blockers,** ie those who might get in your way

It is vital that you influence both these groups and the RACI model will help you to understand who they are.

 The RACI model

The RACI model is mainly used for clarifying and defining roles and responsibilities in organisational, departmental and cross-functional projects, processes or programmes. RACI is an acronym of the four key roles in these activities: responsible, accountable, consulted, and informed.

Using RACI will help you to identify:

- Who is **responsible** for delivering the task / activity that you are communicating about? Who else is working on it?

- Who is **accountable** for it? Who makes the key decisions? Whose head will roll if it isn't successful?

- Who should be **consulted**? Who can tell you more about it? Who can help you to shape your communication?

- Who needs to be kept **informed**? Where are the interdependencies? Whose toes might you be stepping on?

Stakeholder mapping

Any communication, whether it's a one-off or a campaign, will have various individuals or groups who are more or less interested in it, impacted by it, and who have more or less influence over it.

The first step in your communication planning is to identify who they are. Ideally you should involve your client or internal customer in this exercise as they are closest to the subject of the communication and will know best who is involved.

Once you've mapped your stakeholders, you will be able to see clearly what levels of communication involvement they will require and plan accordingly, ie:

- Low interest, low influence – those you need only to inform. Keep in touch with this group, but do not overload them with excessive information or overly frequent communication.

- High interest, low influence – those you need to inform and consult with. These stakeholders can often provide helpful input so keep them regularly informed, seek their input and keep track of any issues or concerns they may have.

- Low interest, high influence – those you need to engage. Maintain active two-way communication, make sure they know their voices are being heard on key issues, but don't turn them off with low value or overly frequent communication.

- High interest, high influence – those you need to engage and collaborate with. These are your key stakeholders from whom you need strong buy-in. You must make every effort to keep them informed, seek their input, listen to what they have to say and be seen to act on it.

Stakeholder mapping exercise

1. Use Post-it notes or an online whiteboard to brainstorm every individual or group who might be interested in or influence your communication.

2. Now, plot your Post-its into four groups on a stakeholder map as follows:

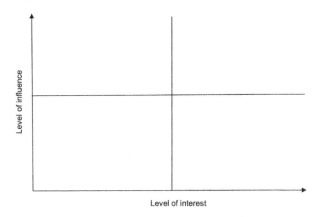

3. Use your completed stakeholder map to help you to decide how best to engage and communicate with each group.

A 'Day in the Life Of' (DILO)

According to *The Sunday Times* (11 April 2021), James Timpson, chief executive of Timpson Group, usually spends three days a week in high streets and retail parks, visiting around 900 of his shops a year, chatting with and listening to colleagues. He believes that 'the more we can travel and meet up to share stories and experiences, the more likely we will be to find new ways to improve our businesses and help our colleagues.'

Timpson was actually the first place I ever worked. I had a Saturday job in their shoe shop in Sunderland, which I loved. These days the shoe shops are long gone. Instead, the group, which employs around 5,000 people, focuses on being shoe repairers, locksmiths, dry cleaners and photo processors, and it consistently ranks in the top ten of *The Sunday Times* '100 Best Companies to Work For'.

Now, spending three days a week out with colleagues may be a stretch, but that doesn't mean you can't put yourself in their shoes (see what I did there). There are other ways to discover what their working world is like, and I find doing a 'Day in the Life Of / Week in the Life Of' exercise helpful.

The 'Day in the Life Of' (DILO) idea was first suggested in a 1994 *Harvard Business Review* article by Francis Gouillart and Frederick D Sturdivant. They suggested that business leaders should be spending a day in the life of their customers to better understand what makes them tick. Of course, the technique works just as well for gaining insight into your internal audiences. It gives a useful understanding of the conditions you're communicating into and how your communications might land with your colleagues.

With internal communication, I've found it's generally more effective to research a Week in the Life Of (WILO). This will give a clearer picture of an average time period – a single day may throw up distortions if it happens to be one that is full of non-standard activities.

The DILO/WILO technique is something I've often used with line managers, as they are the people we rely on for onward communication of our messages to frontline colleagues and for gathering feedback from them. It's easy for us communicators to write into our plans, 'to be onward communicated by line managers', but it is a real eye-opener to see what else they have on their plates and how difficult it is for them to actually deliver what we're expecting of them.

 DILO/WILO Exercise

1. Decide which group you want to understand better, eg line managers or a particular team.

2. Work with one or two of them to identify the broad headings their activities fall under, eg attending meetings, preparing reports, helping customers, etc.

3. Create a form/timesheet with these headings along the top and timings down the side (ideally in a

spreadsheet, so it's easy to add up the totals). See example below.

4. Get a small sample of colleagues to fill in the timesheet for an average day/week.

5. Review findings, understand the implications for your communication, and factor these into your plans.

How many minutes did you spend? Please enter start and finish times.	Activity 1	Activity 2	Activity 3	Activity 4	Activity 5	Activity 6	Etc
0800–1000							
1000–1200							
1200–1400							
1400–1600							
1600–1800							
Other times							
Total							

A typical Day in the Life of (DILO) spreadsheet. Fill one of these in from Monday to Friday and it becomes a Week in the Life of (WILO).

Inbox analysis

Another useful way to gain an understanding of how realistic your communication expectations are of line managers (or any other subsection of your audience) is to do an inbox analysis. Simply select some willing volunteers from the group you are focusing on and ask them, for one week, to forward you anything they get in their inbox that relates to communication.

That might be communications they need to read and understand for themselves, or communications they need to cascade or onward brief – or both. At the end of the week, take a look at what they have sent you.

I guarantee you'll be amazed. I certainly was when I did this exercise with some line managers as part of a communication audit for a rail company. I was surprised – first, by what they sent me, ie, what they consider to be related to communication, and second, by how much they sent me – the sheer quantity of communication requests they were being bombarded with (most of which weren't from the communication department, but from HR, health and safety, finance, operations and all sorts of other teams at a local, regional and national level).

The inbox analysis clearly demonstrated that line managers were being deluged with demands that they had no hope of being able to respond to, especially alongside doing their day jobs. The communications were being set up to fail if they were relying on this group of overstretched employees to read, understand and act on them.

Sharing this insight with leaders proved extremely valuable in helping the penny to drop about the unrealistic expectations that were being set and the need for some 'air traffic control' to help manage the flow, as well as to make what they were receiving shorter, better signposted and easier to respond to.

Personas

The first time I remember coming across personas was when I worked with a major brewer that had a well-known superstrength lager in its portfolio. At the time, these lagers were closely associated with alcohol misuse, so the marketing team did some research to see who was actually drinking the brand and, using this insight, they came up with three distinct personas:

1. **Users** – by far the biggest group, who choose superstrength lager at the beginning of a drinking occasion to get the party started

2. **Connoisseurs** – a smaller group, who enjoy and savour high-strength drinks for their taste, rather than their effect

3. **Abusers** – a very small, but highly visible group, who choose whatever drink will get them the biggest bang for their buck

Twenty years on, I can still remember those personas and how useful they were in targeting the marketing for the brand, as well as in defending its very existence.

Once again, internal communicators can learn from our marketing colleagues, and in recent years, I've seen a rise in the use of personas in internal communication.

Personas are made-up characters who represent sub-sets of your audience. They're a great way to paint a picture in your mind of who your communication is aimed at. The idea is to take what you actually know about your audience, from data and insight, and use this to segment them, based on what they're interested in, how they can be reached, etc.

Once you've gathered your data and insight, it's helpful and fun to create characters to represent the different personas you come up with. For example, if you're segmenting your internal audience by team, department or function, you might have characters like Sabita in Sales, Mo in Marketing or Andy in Accounts.

For groups segmented by attitude, outlook or engagement levels, you might have Engaged Ella, Disillusioned Dev or Saboteur Sam.

Age or career stage make a big difference. If, for example, you're communicating about pensions, you could create a character for each of the recognised generations in the workplace, ie Baby Boomers, Gen X, Millennials and Gen Z.

Another useful way of segmenting your internal audience may be to recognise how their work location or situation impacts their ability to receive your communication, eg Deskless Debbie, Plugged-in Pete, Nightshift Nigel or Mobile Miguel.

Don't go mad though, there's no point in having dozens of personas if you're not actually able to create and deliver communication that is specifically tailored to each of them. Stick with a handful of meaningful personas you want to target in particular. Bring them to life with images and mini-biographies that you can keep to hand and refer to in your communication planning or when sharing your ideas with internal stakeholders.

The personas can be used simply once you've got them. I've worked with companies who applied the 'Dave the Driver' test to all their communication content, asking themselves, what would Dave the Driver make of this? That's a great way to ensure simplicity and clarity for messages where one size fits all, but for more complex or nuanced communications, beware of overly dumbing things down.

That's where your range of personas comes into its own – helping you to tailor your content to the different audiences and ensuring that each gets exactly what they need and what interests them. Going back to the superstrength lager drinkers, if these were internal audiences, you'd focus on the drink's effects for the users, the taste for the connoisseurs and the cost for the abusers (not that you'd ever be targeting this group of course).

Summary

In the past, marketers would view their audiences as one mass group, delivering the same experience to everyone. This made sense when there were fewer choices and less data. However, getting data, insight and opinion from customers has become much easier in recent years and this has led to more bespoke, tailored marketing – mass personalisation. As Travis M Hessman put it in *Industry Week* (2013), 'Today's consumers will no longer accept one-size-fits-all. Nor do they expect it.'

The same applies to internal communication. With more opportunity to get to know our audiences there's no excuse for a one-size-fits-all approach. By putting yourself in the shoes of individual subsets, you can tailor your plans.

Using techniques like stakeholder mapping, RACI, the DILO/WILO, inbox analysis and personas will enable you to answer the Audience questions we outlined earlier with real insight and precision. Applying these techniques will remind you and your key internal stakeholders that everyone is not the same and will help you to plan and implement internal communication strategies that cater for your different audiences.

Musing 2: Marcus Rashford – the importance of authenticity

During the 2020 Covid-19 lockdown, Manchester United striker Marcus Rashford elevated himself from football hero to national hero.

The twenty-two-year-old footballer used his public platform for good. His open letter to MPs, urging the government to reverse a decision not to provide free school meals during the summer holidays, prompted major changes in government policy and that makes him a bit of a rock star in my eyes.

Celebrities who do this sort of thing can come across as people with privilege who are jumping on a bandwagon, so what made Rashford different?

A key factor was his *authenticity*. His messages weren't finessed, but they were real. His TV interviews weren't slick – he was wearing his slippers in the ones I saw – but he came across as genuinely caring. He talked from the heart about his own childhood memories of being hungry. He has been giving back to his community for years, quietly but effectively.

Over the years, I've drafted many letters, speeches, presentations and announcements for business leaders – occasionally even for people I have never met. Although the words were well written and contained all the key corporate messages, these communications only connected with the audiences when the person delivering them *really* meant what they said.

Audiences, especially employees, are great detectors of bullshit.

3
Behaviours

Internal communication adds real value by changing not only employees' opinions but their behaviours too. It's not a soft and fluffy activity that organisations do to make their employees feel happy, and it shouldn't just be something that leaders and managers do so they can tick the communication box. As the Institute of Internal Communication outlines in their mission statement, 'Successful internal communication creates an environment of mutual understanding. It forges connections between people, allowing them to perform at their best, both individually and collectively.'

If your communication results in people changing what they think and what they do in ways that align with what your organisation is trying to achieve, then you will be contributing to its success, however that is measured. Oh, and your people will probably feel happier too – but that is a nice by-product, not the only aim.

Once you've established exactly **who** your communication is aimed at (Audiences), the next questions to ask are:

- Why are you communicating with them? What is the objective?

- What do we want people to do, say, think and feel?

- How can you motivate them to make the required change?

Your internal stakeholders/clients may need some help to answer these questions. Don't be fobbed off with answers like 'I just want them to know about it' – keep asking *why* until you get to the real nub of the situation. In this chapter, we'll explore some techniques you can use to identify what behaviour change you're really trying to achieve.

Most successful communication will lead to behaviour change of some sort. It will generally involve actually doing something different. Even if you're simply telling people the canteen is closed on Friday, what you want is a behaviour change, ie for the canteen-users to make other arrangements.

Employee behaviour, in fact human behaviour, is mainly driven by two things – the desire to get something or the desire to avoid something – in other words, the carrot or the stick. In your communication planning, you should decide which approach you think will be most effective, or you could use a combination of the two. At its simplest, ask whether the message you're communicating to your audience is 'if you make this change, something good will happen', or 'if you don't make this change something bad will happen'. Or is it both?

A useful thing about behaviours is that they are observable and therefore measurable. Behaviours are what you see your employees doing or hear them saying. They are not just what employees are thinking or feeling, they are a visible manifestation of those thoughts or feelings. As a result, this is an important part of the communication planning process. Get this right and you'll have defined your success measures. But more on that in Chapter 6.

As your communication is going to impact behaviours, it helps to understand a little more about them. You don't need a degree in psychology, but it's useful to have a basic understanding of some behaviour theories that you can use to guide your planning.

 **Behaviour theory 1:
The ABC model**

The first model is often used in education or care settings, but it can be applied equally well to business situations. Behavioural psychologist BF Skinner describes it as the 'three-term contingency of operant conditioning', but ABC is easier to remember, and stands for Antecedents, Behaviours and Consequences.

Antecedents

These are the things that come before – the information or events that lead to behaviour change. They can be immediate or an accumulation of previous events or information. They drive behaviour change and are a key part of any communication plan.

Example: You communicate statistics about the increasing rate of workplace accidents, bringing them to life with real examples. This is the trigger for colleagues to change their behaviour.

Behaviours

These are the desired actions, which ideally can be observed and measured. That way, data, rather than assumptions, can be used to influence consequences. The desired behaviours need to be clearly defined in your communication plan.

Example: You ask employees to increase the number of near misses they report so preventative measures can be taken to avoid future workplace accidents. This behaviour change can be observed and measured.

Consequences

These are the positive or negative ways behaviours can be reinforced, such as feedback, rewards, reminders, or even reprimands. They motivate behaviour change and are another important, often forgotten, element of communication planning.

Example: Individuals / teams who increase their reporting are publicly praised, and those who do not are privately reminded. If an overall increase in reporting is observed, this can be used as evidence that the communication was effective. If not, you may need to rethink your strategy.

 ## Behaviour theory 2: The AMP model

In his 2010 book, *Drive: The surprising truth about what motivates us*, Daniel Pink argues that while the carrot and stick approach may work for simple tasks, it is not the best way to motivate employees, especially when they are faced with challenges that require problem-solving, creativity or conceptual understanding. He goes as far as to say the carrot and stick approach is 'incompatible with many aspects of contemporary business'.

Pink suggests that what drives us to deliver high performance in the workplace is a deep desire to direct our own lives, to extend and expand our abilities, and to live a life of purpose. His approach to motivation has three elements: autonomy, mastery and purpose.

Autonomy

This refers to our desire to direct our own lives – the ability to control our own tasks, our time, our techniques and our teams.

Mastery

This is the urge to get better and better at something that matters.

Purpose

This is the yearning to do what we do in the service of something larger than ourselves.

This technique involves engaging employees to come up with and apply their own solutions, rather than these coming top-down from management. For example, you could run some focus groups or workshops with teams where the accident rate has been increasing, and ask them, 'What do you think we should do to help us get better at making sure everyone gets home safely every day?' This would provide an opportunity for employees to experience autonomy (what do you think), mastery (help us get better) and purpose (making sure everyone gets home safely).

This approach will require more involvement and, as such, more time, but it will deliver a better result in terms of employee engagement. The participants might come up with the same solution as management, or they may come up with other ideas. Either way, they are more likely to be motivated if they are given the opportunity to solve the problem for themselves.

Given that, you might wonder why I bothered telling you about the ABC model of behaviour. Well, there are plenty of occasions when the ABC model can still usefully be applied. Perhaps the communication is urgent and you simply haven't got time to involve your people, or maybe your people don't want to be involved because they haven't got time, or if their trade unions discourage it. It could even be that a more engaging approach like the AMP model is a step too far for your organisational culture. Your organisation may not be ready for such a collaborative approach, in which case, you'll need to recognise this and do what you can inside the cultural parameters of the business.

 **Audience View Exercise**

As communicators, we generally think about behaviours from our own point of view, ie what we want employees

to start/stop or do more/less of as a result of our communication. But it is useful to think about them from the employees' point of view. Ask yourself:

- What will encourage or prevent employees from embracing the change I am seeking?
- Will they be motivated by an 'if–then' approach or by being more involved?
- How will they know what is expected of them?
- How will they know if/when they are doing the right things?

Use your responses to help shape your communication plan.

If you're interested in what motivates and engages people at work and want to find out more, I recommend you take a look at *Employee Engagement: An evidence review* published by CIPD in January 2021. It covers four key areas that are commonly associated with employee engagement:

- Work engagement – whether people feel vigorous, dedicated and absorbed in their work

- Organisational commitment – in particular looking at employees' psychological feelings

- Organisational identification – how employees psychologically associate with their organisations

- Work motivation – factors that lead people to be interested in and committed to their job

Behaviour change: The ICE model

An important part of communication planning is defining your objective. This is where you ask what you want people to do, say, think or feel as a result of your communication. To achieve actual behaviour change (the doing), you will need to take your audience through the three stages of being informed, connected and engaged. At this point, it's worth reminding yourself and your stakeholders that this is usually a cumulative process. It's very hard to leap directly to 'engaged'.

The ICE model is a useful way to identify what behaviour change you want as a result of your communication and to express your answers in a way that will inform your communication planning.

Informed

When an employee is informed, they have gained an understanding. As a communicator, you have influenced what they *think*. An informed employee may say to you, 'I get it' or 'I know about it.' For simple announcements, for example about changes to systems, processes or procedures, this may be all that is required.

Connected

When an employee is connected, they have changed their mindset and have bought in to what you have to say. You have influenced what they *feel*. A connected employee may say, 'I like it' or 'I want to play my part.' When communicating about fundamental things like a new vision, a culture change or your employer experience you will be aiming to achieve this.

Engaged

When an employee is engaged, their behaviour has changed and they are doing things differently. You have influenced what they *do*. An engaged employee will tell you, 'I know what's needed' or 'I'm doing my bit.' This is your ultimate outcome. You need to fully engage people to change their behaviour – for example, when you want to 'turn strategy into action' or you need them to 'live the values'.

There's more about using the ICE model to inform your communication planning in Chapter 5.

 **Behaviour measurement: The SMART model**

You are probably familiar with this model, as SMART objectives are used widely in other business practices such as project management and performance management. SMART became popular in the 1980s following a 1981 *Management Review* article by George Doran. Setting SMART objectives is an effective tool for communication planning as it ensures that you and/or your stakeholders give proper consideration to what you are aiming to achieve. The model also helps you to define your objectives clearly and in a way that can be revisited in the evaluation stage. This is vital to prove your communication has worked.

Specific

Being specific means being clear about exactly who is involved in your communication, what the aim is, where it will happen, when it will happen, and why you're doing it.

Measurable

To make your communication measurable, you need to decide what criteria you will use to evaluate your success. This will usually involve numbers, eg how many more near-miss reports/fewer accidents? What percentage improvement?

Achievable

The objective of your communication needs to be realistic. Do your employees have the resources, capability or time to attain your objective? There's no point in setting them up to fail.

Relevant

Your communication must be relevant and its objective must support or align with your organisation's vision, strategy, values and goals.

Time-bound

You need to establish a realistic deadline or time frame in which your objective needs to be delivered. This will create a sense of urgency and encourage employees to take action.

Let's say the safety manager has told you that there should typically be eight to ten near misses for every real accident, according to safety theory. But there are currently only two near misses being reported for every real accident. The safety manager believes that near misses are going unreported, so learning is not being captured. This means that preventative measures are not being put in place to ensure that near misses don't become real accidents.

If you were asked to help with a communication campaign to increase near-miss reporting, your SMART objective might be:

- The operations team will increase the number of near misses they report. (Specific)

- They will do this weekly using the existing near-miss form and reporting process. (Achievable)

- This will align with the company's 'Zero Harm' policy. (Relevant)

- In six months, there will be eight times as many near-miss reports as there are actual accidents. (Time-bound and Measurable)

Summary

At its heart, internal communication is about encouraging employees to do the right things and to display the right behaviours. As you've seen, there are two key aspects of behaviour to consider in your communication planning.

One is to clearly define the behaviour change your communication is aiming to achieve. For this, you need to ask the first two questions set out at the beginning of this chapter, use the ICE model to help answer them, and then set SMART objectives to define the results.

The other aspect to consider is behaviour theory – having an understanding of what will motivate your employees to make the behaviour change you are seeking, and, of course, what might prevent them from doing so. This is where the third question comes in: how can you motivate them to make the required change? You can use the ABC model or the AMP model for this, depending on which best suits your organisational culture.

By taking time to consider both of these factors, you will be gathering valuable input for your communication plan. You and your key stakeholders will be completely clear and aligned on exactly what outcome you are seeking, and you'll have identified a measurable objective so you will be able to demonstrate your success when your aim is achieved.

Musing 3: Rock Against Racism – campaign for something, not against

Seeing the Black Lives Matter protests following the murder of George Floyd in May 2020 reminded me of my student days, when we marched against apartheid and rocked against racism.

The Rock Against Racism movement brought together black and white music fans to stop the rise of the National Front, an extreme right-wing political party that was against non-white immigration and multiculturalism.

Rock Against Racism directly influenced the formation of multicultural bands like The Beat, UB40 and The Specials – still some of my favourite live bands ever. At the time, it was unusual to see a mix of white and black band members and a mix of white and black fans. Forty years on, integration has improved, but sadly, ignorance and intolerance continues.

As a communicator, I've always recommended campaigning *for* something rather than against, so maybe now is the time for a new movement – Music for Multiculturalism, anyone?

4

Content

William Penn, the British writer, founder of Pennsylvania, and supposedly the original Quaker on the Quaker Oats box, understood as far back as the seventeenth century that communication is not about being clever – it's about being clear. His advice was: 'Speak properly, and in as few words as you can, but always plainly; for the end of speech is not ostentation, but to be understood.' But that's not enough. Whether it is spoken or written, audio or visual, your content also needs to be compelling, in context and, ideally, concise. Your role as a communicator is to make sure that the ideas you're trying to convey to your audiences are received, understood and acted on.

Once you've established exactly **who** your communication is aimed at (Audiences) and **why** you are communicating with them (Behaviours), you need to create your Content.

The next questions to consider are:

- What key messages do you want to convey?

- Will your content connect? Is it clear, compelling, in context and concise?

- Is your role to create, co-create or curate the content?

Don't forget, channels of communication may be *how* our audiences connect with us, but content is *why*. Content is king. It needs to inform, connect with and engage your audience, or even the fanciest channels in the world won't reach them.

What, so what and now what?

Your focus at this stage of your planning is on what content you need to include and, as importantly, what you should leave out. For this, I particularly like the simplicity of Steve Crescenzo's approach. Crescenzo is a former journalist who is now a well-known communication speaker, workshop leader, consultant and coach. He recommends asking three questions:

1. **What?** What does your audience need to know?

2. **So what?** Why should they care?

3. **Now what?** What do you want them to do
   differently?

It's as simple as that. When you've got the answer
to those three questions, you can then begin crafting
your content in a way that will cut through to your
audience. For this, try applying the Six C test.

 **The Six C test**

This is a simple test you can apply to make sure you're
getting it right. There are six questions to ask yourself:

1. Will your content connect?

2. Is it clear?

3. Is it compelling?

4. Is it in context?

5. Is it concise?

6. Is it channel-specific?

Let's take a look at each of these in turn.

1. Will your content connect?

A great way to connect with your audience is to be as
open and honest as possible. Tell people as much as
possible, as soon as possible. If your communication

is about *not* being able to tell them something, explain why and say when you will be able to.

Treat your audience like adults. Don't talk to them like a parent to a child. Speak to them like peers, respect them, and never underestimate their intelligence.

As discussed in Chapter 2, understanding your audience is vital. When you know who you're communicating with, you can show empathy and compassion. By doing so, you will build confidence and trust.

But beware, trust can easily be lost if your communication is not perceived to be authentic. Being authentic is more important than being perfect. People will overlook a wobbly, homemade video if the person in it sounds like they're speaking from the heart.

2. Is it clear?

People are busy. There is a lot competing for their attention. Help your audience to see the wood for the trees by making your communication as clear as possible. To do this you should:

- Make sure you're writing in everyday language. Avoid what I call 'business bollocks'. Write it as you speak, using short sentences and avoiding jargon and acronyms.

- Read what you've written out loud and honestly assess if the words are what you or your audience would actually use in real life. As Crescenzo advises, write for the reader, not the approver.

- Check your readability statistics. You can do this in software such as Microsoft Word or via websites such as Grammarly or Readable.

- Make it clear to your audience what is expected of them. Give them some simple instructions or signposting, such as 'read this', 'share this' or 'action this'.

3. Is it compelling?

Another of Crescenzo's tips is to think about how to 'make the important interesting'.

To do that, you should avoid writing about what he calls the 'deadly Ps' – things like programmes, products, processes, policies and procedures. No matter how passionate your internal stakeholders are about these things, no matter how much they want you to share their latest milestone plan or spreadsheet, you need to persuade them that other people simply aren't that interested in them.

What people are interested in is other people, so focus on finding people-centred stories to bring the deadly

Ps to life. Real-life examples and case studies will help your audiences to connect with what is really important in your content, and avoid them turning off as soon as they see the deadly P-words appear.

Think about what people pay to read – they buy books and newspapers to be entertained or educated through storytelling. Speaking at an East Midlands Internal Communications professionals' virtual networking event on 29 September 2020, Rachael Bull of business storytelling company Write the Talk identified the following of types of stories that are commonly found in literature, films and news:

- Origin stories
- Overcoming monsters
- Rags to riches/triumph of the underdog
- Quest stories/journeys
- Rebirth stories

These can also work well for internal communication and can help you create compelling content to engage your audience. Instead of telling employees the details of your change programme, for example, excite them about the journey they're embarking on and paint a picture of the destination that is so captivating, it's well worth the pain of getting there.

4. Is it in context?

Have you ever received a laminated card, a lanyard, a mug or a mousemat with the latest company vision, values or strategic priorities printed on them? For some employees, often those on the frontline, who are closest to the customer, that is all they get.

To get to the point of issuing these items, a small number of the most senior people in the organisation may have spent several months working with external consultants, exploring and discussing options, reviewing business objectives and agreeing messages. These senior people get the need for change, they understand it and are fully bought in. They're raring to go. It's easy for them to forget that the rest of the organisation is not there yet. Everyone else needs time to catch up – they need to understand the thought processes that have led to the outcomes, to have the context for the change explained to them. Instead, they just get the laminated card and are expected to change their behaviour just like that.

It's your job as a communication professional to help your leaders see the error of their ways, to recognise how ludicrous it is to expect Dave the Driver, or indeed anyone else in the organisation, to do anything differently without anyone taking the time to explain or involve and engage him in doing so.

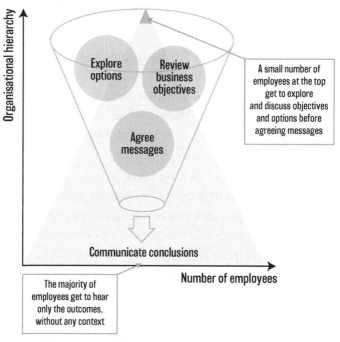

The context funnel©

Showing them the context funnel might help. I've used it for years to help make this important point to senior leaders, to remind them of their privileged position and of the need to bring others with them on the journey.

5. Is it concise?

Storytelling and context are important, but there are times when it's more important just to get to the point. This is especially true for frontline and non-desk-based colleagues. They have limited time to access and digest your communication, so avoid long preambles and don't bury the important bit several paragraphs in. Just answer the three 'what' questions outlined above as quickly and clearly as possible.

You can always provide access to more details for those who have the time or the inclination to read more, but make sure you are helping those in a hurry to see the wood for the trees.

6. Is it channel-specific?

I'll be looking at channels in more detail in the next chapter, but from a content point of view, it is vital to tailor your content to your channel. What works for face-to-face or verbal channels will not necessarily be right for online, and vice versa.

So don't be tempted to just create one version of your narrative and use it everywhere. As is often the case in internal communication, one size does not fit all.

Visual content

It's often said that a picture paints a thousand words, and that is certainly true when it comes to internal communication. Impactful imagery, great graphics and meaningful materials can help your message cut through. Pictures will often become visual shortcuts for your communication – they stick in your audience's minds, triggering recognition, encouraging conversation, and aiding understanding and buy-in.

But beware. Those benefits apply only to the right images. Get it wrong and you risk distracting or even annoying your audience. Whether you're considering using still images (such as slides, pictures, diagrams, charts, infographics, photographs, illustrations or icons) or moving images (such as videos, gifs or animations), you need to put as much careful thought into their creation as you do for your words.

For the images you're considering, ask yourself the following questions:

1. Are they adding value for your audience, or do you not need them?

2. Do they support your key messages or distract from them?

3. Are they easy to understand, or are they open to misinterpretation?

4. Are they representative of your audience – inclusive or not exclusive?

5. Do they oversimplify or dumb down complex messages?

6. And finally, from a practical point of view, is your audience able to access them?

Is your role to create, co-create or curate the content?

A key part of any communicator's role is to create content. You are expected to craft the perfect written or spoken words to convey information, ideas and instructions effectively. Much of this chapter has focused on equipping you to do that.

You will find, however, that it is not always best to create content yourself. Involving employees in co-creating content will make them feel more connected to the message and, as a result, they'll be more likely to understand and act on it.

And increasingly, the communicator's role is not to just to craft content, but also to curate and moderate the content and conversations of others. As a curator, you will want to allow, and indeed encourage, as many people as possible to contribute their own content to fuel the conversation. Any natural storytellers in your organisations should be encouraged to tell their stories and champion others to do the same.

Your role will then be that of moderator to ensure their content aligns with the organisation's strategy, goals and values. This will require the provision of effective two-way channels of communication (more on this in Chapter 5), but even with these in place, conversation will only thrive if you are able to build a sense of community. This is a massive topic in its own right. There is even an annual Community Manager Advancement Day – the fourth Monday in January – which recognises and celebrates the efforts of community managers and provides resources and advice, including events and ebooks, for those wanting to improve their skills.

Laurence McCahill, co-founder of The Happy Startup, points out the value of a community in comparison to a mere audience: 'Don't confuse building an audience with building a community. One is about you – growing your customer base. The other is about them — creating true connection between the people you're serving. You become less important, merely a catalyst.'

As a moderator, your role is more of a gatekeeper, or maybe an air traffic controller. You need to establish and enforce reasonable and consistent communication protocols to ensure that communication content is appropriate and channels are being used effectively.

To avoid the conversation becoming chaotic and to ensure your audiences aren't overloaded or overwhelmed, you should:

- Create a communication calendar, so people know when to expect certain communications, eg a news roundup on a Friday, or a leadership vlog the first week of every month

- Be consistent about the channels used for your different types of content

For more on channels, see Chapter 5.

Summary

People have a short attention span and it's getting shorter. A 2015 report by Microsoft Canada showed that the average human attention span had reduced from twelve seconds in 2000 to just eight seconds in 2015 – and claimed that this was less than a goldfish! Even back in 1978, Nobel prize winner Herbert Simon noted that 'a wealth of information creates a poverty of attention.' As a result, it's critical that your content cuts through and lands with your audience in the way it was intended.

Once you have explored the three key 'Content' questions of the ABCDE model, you will know what is expected of you and will be able to deliver accordingly.

But if the default is always for you to create, you may need to introduce your internal stakeholders to the benefits of co-creation and curation as effective ways to involve and engage colleagues.

Musing 4: Penetration – Shout Above the Noise

Springwatch presenter Chris Packham is a closet punk. He posts a playlist on Twitter with the hashtag #punkrockmidnight and recently, he played a punk band called Penetration. They were the first band I ever saw live and that experience literally changed my life. As a teenager, I was a big fan, going to their gigs, buying every record they released and playing them on repeat – even ill-advisedly wearing their T-shirt for my passport photo (resulting in ten years of raised eyebrows at border control).

What was the appeal? Well, they were local, showing you didn't have to live in the London to be in a band. They had a gorgeous and edgy singer, Pauline Murray. But most of all, their songs really resonated with my teenage self. They were about not being told what to do or who to be ('Don't Dictate'), celebrating people who are different ('Lovers of Outrage'), and speaking out and making yourself heard ('Shout Above the Noise'). In fact, the messages in their songs still resonate today.

5

Delivery

Too many communication conversations start with the channel – there seems to be a complete obsession with having the latest bit of technology and with every team, every project and every territory having their own channels. This leads to audience overload and confusion, and leaves internal communicators with the impossible task of trying to co-ordinate communication delivery when they have very little or no control over who is saying what, when, how and to whom.

On Masgroves' *Pull No Punches* podcast, internal communication guru Bill Quirke described internal communicators as being 'seduced' by channels. He went on to explain that 'the value is not in the channels, it's in the thinking.' I couldn't agree more. This chapter is all about the thinking – the questions you need to ask to help you to decide how best to deliver your communication.

After, and *only* after, you've established exactly **who** your communication is aimed at (Audiences), **why** you are communicating with them (Behaviours), and **what** you are communicating (Content), can you start to think about **how** you communicate (Delivery). To do this, you should ask:

- What channels should you choose? Verbal, online or print?

- Do you need to build your line managers' or leaders' communication capability?

- Do you have enough two-way channels? Are you really listening?

Choosing your channels

Internal communicators have never had so many channels to choose from – so where do you start? All the work you have already done in the ABCDE model, identifying your audiences, the behaviour changes you're seeking and the content you want to convey, will help to inform which channels you choose. The ICE model introduced in Chapter 3 can also help you to decide on your delivery method.

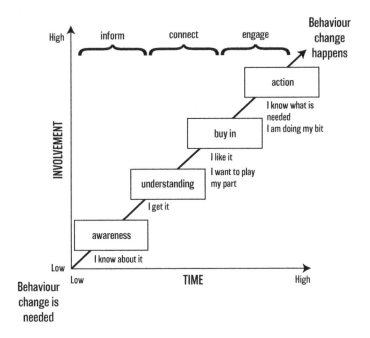

The ICE model© helps you choose channels

If you only want to *inform* your audience, this will require very little time and involvement. To simply provide information, use awareness channels that you know will reach your identified audiences. These will be one-way 'tell' channels, ie those designed to inform, such as apps, intranet, emails, posters, newsletters, podcasts or videos. These are also mainly pull channels, which colleagues can self-serve at a time that suits them. Some of these channels also serve as the go-to place for business/job critical information, such as policies and forms, which everyone should be able to access easily, on demand.

To *connect* with your audience will require a bit more time and a bit more involvement. For this you should use two-way channels that you know will reach your identified audiences. These channels will encourage a bit more dialogue and might include conferences, meetings, townhalls, webinars and huddles. These are mainly push channels, which are delivered at a particular time and place (although they can also be recorded and made available on demand). They generally involve groups of employees coming together, in real life or virtually, to be briefed and given an opportunity to ask questions. They can be followed up with further information provided through the pull channels identified above, or with things like pulse surveys to gather feedback and quizzes/competitions to reinforce understanding.

Finally, to engage with your audience, you will need to *involve* them, and this will inevitably take more time. For this, you need two-way channels that are more about listening than telling. These might include workshops, focus groups, employee forums, special interest groups and skip level meetings. Two-way channels like these provide opportunities for those present to participate in dialogue, make valued suggestions, contribute ideas and shape outcomes.

Having conducted many communication audits over the years, I know that most organisations are well off for one-way 'tell' channels. The trouble is that often the leaders of these organisations – and sometimes even their communicators – think that because they've got all these channels, and because they are so busy feeding them with content, they have ticked the internal communication box. All it really means, though, is that you've done the easy, tactical bit. If you want to deliver value-adding, strategic communication, you need to ensure that you also have plenty of effective channels to connect and engage with your audiences. They are where the real communication happens – the communication that results in behaviour change. You should spend a large proportion of your time and effort on these, and not a disproportionate amount of time and effort on simply informing people. For more about operating strategically, see Chapter 8.

 Channel Mapping Exercise

1. Identify all your existing channels of internal communication.

2. Plot your channels onto the channel map below.

3. Use your completed channel map as a menu to help you decide which channels best suit which communications/audiences.

4. Use your channel map to identify where you might have too many or too few channels.

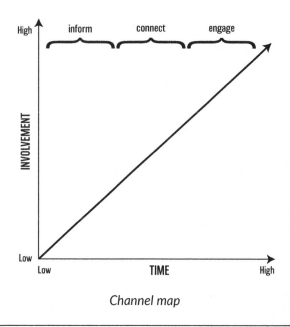

Channel map

Verbal communication

Verbal communication happens when we speak with others. This can be face-to-face, in real life, via an audio platform such as a phone, radio or podcast, or via virtual platforms such as Teams, Skype or Zoom. It can be live or recorded for playback on demand. It can be one-way or two-way. Some verbal communication is informal, such as chatting with a colleague in the canteen or the corridor – these are the so-called 'water cooler moments'. Other verbal communication in the workplace is more formal, such as meetings, townhalls, webinars and huddles – the key channels we use to *connect* with our colleagues. Formal communication can also include workshops, focus groups, employee forums, special interest groups and skip level meetings – the key channels we use to *engage* with our colleagues.

You have control, or at least influence, over some of the formal communication channels. You have no control over the informal channels, although if your formal channels are working effectively, they may influence what is talked about in those water cooler moments.

The key to successful verbal communication is the people who are delivering it – and this is usually your leaders and line managers. As well as being key audiences for your communication, I'd argue they are also your most important channels. As such, an important, often overlooked, part of your role is to establish and build the communication capability of your leaders and line managers.

Building line manager communication capability

For most employees, their go-to person for communication is their line manager. As a result, when planning communication, it's common to allocate communication responsibilities to line managers – you may have done this by sending something out as 'to be cascaded by line managers', with the instruction, 'Line managers to gather feedback', or telling employees, 'For further information ask your line manager.'

There is an assumption that line managers are willing and able to do these things, but as you will have probably experienced, their communication capability can vary greatly. A Melcrum white paper, *Innovation and Intervention in Manager Communication*, showed that while 86% of managers think their communication performance is 'good to very good', 83% of employees rated their managers' communication ability as only 'poor to average'. In addition, Towers Watson found that only 40% of frontline managers were able to understand and explain key organisational decisions, rising to 53% of mid-level managers and 68% of senior managers.

Part of the problem is that, although line managers are given responsibility for communication, they are generally not given any accountability for it. It's not something that is routinely included in their KPIs, and it's not usually measured, rewarded or improved via training. Indeed, Melcrum found that fewer than 30% of large companies had defined any communication competencies for their line managers and only one in five were measuring the communication performance of managers. The same survey showed that 54% don't offer any communication training to managers at all and that those who do tend only to offer tactical training on things like presentation skills.

With this in mind, rather than asking, 'What can my line managers do for me?', you should be asking, 'What can I do for my line managers?' The Local Government Association offers some great advice on this, which I've summarised and built on below:

1. Don't just give line managers another task to add to their already long to-do list, eg 'cascade this'. Explain exactly what you expect of them and what the benefits will be.

2. Make what you are asking them to do as simple as possible by providing them with easy access to the right advice, information and materials, eg toolkits.

3. Give them something extra, such as early access to information, so they can get prepared, or FAQs, so they are equipped to answer follow-up questions.

4. Offer them formal communication training and development and provide them with coaching or mentoring opportunities, either from internal communication specialists, or from colleagues who are doing a good job.

5. Involve them early in your planning – test your ideas on them, seek their input, listen to their concerns, then build and adjust your plans accordingly.

6. Co-ordinate what you are communicating with others, so line managers aren't bombarded with multiple asks at once.

7. Forward plan so you can give line managers plenty of notice, taking into account practicalities like holidays, shifts and seasonality, as well as other work priorities they may have.

In addition to the above ideas, you and your HR colleagues should make sure that line managers know that communication is an important part of their role and ensure that rewards and recognition are in place for those who are embracing it. On the flip side, it can be effective to have visible consequences for those who aren't.

Building leadership communication capability

All the advice in the previous section about line manager communication can also be applied to leadership communication. But as well as being an important channel of communication, leaders also have a key role to play in employee engagement.

John Smythe, a pioneering thought leader in organisational communication, went as far as to redefine the CEO's role as Chief Engagement Officer, describing its main duties as:

- Advocating the company's vision

- Focusing people on the right work

- Knowing and delivering what engages people

- Power sharing – considering who to engage in decision-making and execution, and governing it well

- Being authentic – having insight and exercising discipline about their personal communication style and tone

- Having attractive values, including fairness and transparency

- Oh, and being good at their day job!

Not every leader, or leadership team, ticks all those boxes, but it is your role as their trusted advisor to help them recognise the importance of this element of their role and to build their capability and confidence as both effective communicators and engagement officers.

There's more about your role as a trusted advisor in Chapter 8, but as part of the delivery stage of your communication planning there are two key considerations when it comes to leaders' role in communication and engagement. Both relate to Engage for Success's key enablers. The first focuses specifically on talking the talk, the second on walking the talk.

Talking the talk

Your leaders must be able to tell a clear, concise and compelling story about the organisation. This is likely to include where it has come from, where it is now, where it is headed and the role your employees will play in getting it there. You need to work with your leaders to define and articulate this narrative, so it is something that they can all buy into and share with their teams. Sounds simple. It isn't.

This is the perfect opportunity for co-creation. Tablets of stone passed down from on high may have worked in biblical times, but nowadays it's more effective to involve as many people as you can. That doesn't mean it's a free-for-all. In general, the most senior team will have the most say in defining the direction of the organisation and in shaping the strategy, but the more you can persuade them to involve others, to listen to and incorporate their ideas, the more buy-in they're likely to get. The context funnel in Chapter 4 may help with this.

Once the narrative is defined, your role is to help your leaders share it in the most impactful and engaging way. If you are launching a new vision, values or strategy you will need to use two-way channels which enable you to connect and engage with your audience. These may already exist, or you may need to create new, bespoke channels. Ideally these will be co-created and delivered by the leadership team to guarantee buy-in and ownership.

Walking the talk

Once you have launched your narrative, it's important to keep walking the talk. Or, as Andy Barrow, former captain of Team GB Paralympic rugby team says, to make sure the 'words on the walls are reflected in the behaviours in the halls'. As with many things in internal communication, you can't expect this just to happen. You have to structure it in. And you can't do it alone – you will probably need some support from HR.

From a behaviours point of view, your HR colleagues should be able to work with your leaders to assess their capabilities and the impact they are having on their teams. They can do this via things like 360° surveys and personality-type tests. The results of these can be used to design learning and development programmes to ensure the leaders are building their communication and engagement skills and learning how to walk the talk.

At the same time, from an internal communication point of view, you can be structuring in numerous opportunities for them to apply these skills. These predominantly two-way channels will help to build leaders' visibility and reinforce their key messages, as well as providing them with valuable opportunities to listen to feedback and tune in to what their colleagues are saying, thinking and doing.

Engage for Success suggests some great ways to do this, which I've summarised and expanded into a *walk-the-talk top ten* below:

1. A 'getting to know you' or 'five minutes with' picture story or video, where leaders can share with their colleagues a bit about their job, who they are and what they like doing.

2. A regular blog or vlog, where leaders can tell staff about their activities, thoughts and ideas. Ideally leaders should write this themselves and provide opportunity for feedback.

3. A real or virtual open-door session or surgery, where leaders make themselves available so that colleagues can book a slot to talk to them about any issue.

4. A briefing/team conversation to share key updates and messages – ideally with bullet points that can be cascaded to a wider audience.

5. A live, virtual or on-demand face-to-face all-hands meeting to discuss things like organisational objectives, change, performance and values – ideally with the opportunity for chat or Q&As.

6. Site visits or walkabouts to reinforce key messages and to hear first-hand about frontline issues and ideas. These need to be scheduled and leaders given realistic targets to make sure these happen.

7. Adult-to-adult conversations – leaders meet with small groups of staff (ten to fifteen people) to exchange stories and work ambitions, or to discuss key topics, such as customer service or safety.

8. Breakfast with the boss/lunch with the leader – as above, but with food.

9. Back-to-the-floor sessions, where leaders spend time carrying out the everyday duties of operational staff to get a real insight into their challenges.

10. Skip level meetings, where leaders can meet with small groups of employees that are more than one step down the chain of command from them. These provide opportunities to ask questions and listen to feedback.

 Walk the Talk Exercise

Ask yourself:

1. How many of the walk-the-talk top ten are happening in your organisation? Are they *really* happening? How could they be improved?

2. What other channels from the walk-the-talk top ten could you introduce? What, if anything, is stopping you from doing so? What can you do to remove or overcome those hurdles?

3. What other, or better, two-way channels could
    you put in place to increase opportunities for your
    leaders to be visible and to listen?

 ## Delivering live communication – advice from the experts

Delivering live communication has always been both
challenging and rewarding. Following these ten top
tips from MediaMaker, a full-service media production company that I have worked with many times,
will help you to get it right:

1. **Be clear on deadlines and budgets**
    Deadlines and budgets are important parameters
    that often dictate the way a project is fulfilled.
    Find out how much time and money you have
    upfront so you can cut your cloth accordingly.
    It's no good proposing a Rolls Royce solution
    if there's only a Ford Fiesta budget (and vice
    versa).

2. **Be equipped**
    It always helps to have the right skills and
    resources to call on. Whether it's in-house
    or external, knowing that you have access to
    creative, strategic, technical and logistical experts
    gives you confidence that what you're promising
    will be delivered.

3. **Be innovative**

   There's always something new happening in
   this space. In recent years, traditional design
   and delivery methods for live events have
   been supplemented with digital. Creators and
   producers who like a challenge have embraced
   and adapted to these developments and are
   using them to create new and exciting ways to
   deliver great communication.

4. **Be curious**

   Depending on where you are in the ICE
   model, there is not a single perfect solution
   for your ambition, but several ways to build
   momentum, make connections and keep people
   engaged in your plans. The more you observe
   and are involved in how people communicate
   in business, the more you understand how
   audiences respond to different formats.

5. **Be brief**

   Today's audiences have less time and patience,
   combined with greater expectations and a need
   to be 'wowed'. The abundance of on-screen
   information has built this expectation, and
   communicators are now competing for attention
   with multiple other channels. Brevity is key.

6. **Be bold**

   In-house channels of communication, such as
   intranet, email and social media, are now the
   norm, but to stand out and deliver 'make a

difference' moments, a change in approach is required – not just another Zoom meeting! This is where experts come in, using their range of experience and specialist knowledge to suggest approaches that you may not have been aware of or even considered possible.

7. Be engaging

Whatever the occasion, great results come from understanding the audience and making the chosen channels work for them. Creating a live and/or digital solution that people enjoy engaging with is the first step. The content can then be brought to life with images, video, animation and attractive text formats. Mixing formats and blending styles of communication will always give the audience a reason to stay engaged, and while it will challenge the communicator, this approach is more likely to meet or exceed expectations.

8. Be curious

Start by asking the right questions. Who are your audience? What do you know about them, ie workplace, hours, devices, interests/ responsibilities? Are you informing them, connecting with them or encouraging engagement? What tools or channels do you have available to you? What does success look like? The answers to all these questions build the roadmap to ensuring that the right messages get to the right people, and in a format that they will engage with.

9. **Be authentic**

Don't look at what others are doing and assume it will work for you. Make sure what you're delivering is true to the style and tone of your organisation and your leaders.

10. **Be measured**

Set clear objectives upfront, then measure your success against these. This will allow you to show what impact your live event has actually had and if it has delivered what it set out to.

Online communication

Online communication can be delivered in various ways, ranging from well-established online channels, such as email and intranets, to the latest AI-driven employee apps. In fact, there's never been so many channels to choose from, including:

- Enterprise social networks (ESNs)
- Apps
- Podcasts
- Collaboration sites
- Instant messaging

- Blogs/vlogs

- Polls

- Digital signage/screens

- Streaming audio/video

- Wikis

- Video-sharing sites/channels

- Text messages

- Meeting platforms such as Zoom, Teams and Google Meet

Many of these channels can be integrated with one another. There are also omnichannel platforms, such as Poppulo, that enable you to plan, personalise, publish and measure your internal communications across multiple digital channels.

Whatever channel (or omnichannel) you choose, the most important thing to always remember is that technology is the servant, not the master. As the ABCDE model demonstrates, you need to understand your audiences, behaviours and content *before* deciding on the best delivery channel. That way, you will have a clear understanding of the purpose of the channel, ie what employee communication requirement it needs to meet. For example, are you looking for a platform where work will happen, such as Teams, or a platform such as Workplace, where people can talk about work and about other things like wellbeing, diversity, equity and inclusion, charity, community, etc?

If the answer is an online channel, the question is then which one will best meet your requirements? Of course, there is no silver bullet and one size does not fit all, but you can take steps to narrow down the field.

Once you have a good idea of what your requirements are there will be no shortage of suppliers claiming they can meet them. It's a complex and ever-growing marketplace, with hundreds of potential solutions for you to choose from.

Assessing apps

The *Gartner Report* is often cited as the go-to place for an independent assessment of the latest apps, and this is true, but their report covers all apps, not just employee apps. For a more specialist view, try the *Employee Apps Report V1.1*, published by ClearBox Consulting in June 2021. The employee apps reviewed in the report provide some or all of the following:

- A tool to share news and information

- A platform for users to talk to one another

- A place to build a sense of community and encourage engagement

- A way to simplify working practices

A user-centric approach

If the solution you identify is something beyond ubiquitous and well-understood channels such as email or intranet, then you need to take a user-centric approach to its design and delivery. This means that you should involve your users in both how it is configured and how it is implemented. By involving users in this way, you are much more likely to get their buy-in.

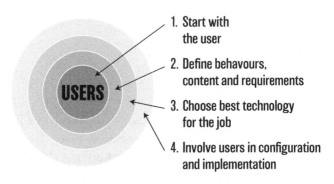

1. Start with the user

2. Define behaviours, content and requirements

3. Choose best technology for the job

4. Involve users in configuration and implementation

User-centric approach©

Taking a technology-led approach, on the other hand, will leave you with the task of selling it to users once it is implemented. This will, at best, result in a time lag in adoption and might, at worst, lead to rejection and with employees coming up with their own workarounds.

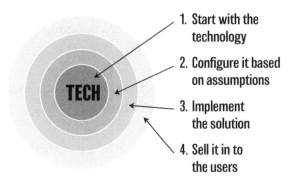

1. Start with the technology

2. Configure it based on assumptions

3. Implement the solution

4. Sell it in to the users

Technology-led approach©

The benefits of online communication

If you have properly identified the need for an on-line channel, understood its purpose, chosen the right product and fully involved your employees in designing and delivering it, then you will be able to enjoy many benefits. From an internal communicator's point of view, the advantages of the latest types of online communication are that they:

- Are data rich, so you can see exactly what is landing and with whom

- De-centralise communication, enabling cross-fertilisation of communication, up, down and across organisations

- Enable you to maintain centralised governance

- Can often be applied across multiple channels, so you can reach even the hardest-to-reach audiences

- Allow you to adapt quickly to changing circumstances or new data

From an employee's perspective, effective channels of online communication enable them to:

- Access communication via a device of their choice

- Self-serve their communication when it suits them

- Share their own stories and comments, giving them a voice

- Browse and select from lots of optional subscriptions (opting in and out)

- Allow artificial intelligence to make recommendations for them

Building a business case

Establishing an online communication channel – or indeed any communication channel – can have significant upfront and ongoing costs, so you will need to a build a business case and show a return on investment. Sharing the benefits for communicators and colleagues that I've outlined above will be part of this,

but other useful tactics could include some or all of
the following:

- **Demonstrate demand** – Are your employees
  asking for this? Are they creating their own
  workarounds because they haven't got it? Are
  there pockets of employees who have already
  successfully adopted it? If not, could you run a
  mini-pilot to help demonstrate the value add?

- **Identify savings** – As a result of implementing
  your new channel, will you be able to stop doing
  something else and save on outgoings. For
  example, could the new channel replace a more
  costly printed publication?

- **Present quantitative benefits** – Can you measure
  any of the benefits in quantitative terms, eg time
  savings, headcount savings, fewer workplace
  accidents, etc?

- **Show risk reduction** – Are your employees
  using their own ungoverned channels such as
  WhatsApp to communicate? If so, that could
  present risks such as security of commercially
  sensitive information or reputational damage.

- **Spread cost** – Could you start small, maybe in
  one team or region? This could mean a smaller
  initial investment and would provide you with
  an opportunity to demonstrate benefits through
  quantitative and qualitative feedback.

- **Cite competitors** – Are your competitors already using this and can you show it is giving them edge? Or are they not, in which case, can you show it will give your organisation a competitor or first-mover advantage?

 ## Golden rules for online communication platforms

Back in the 1990s, when I worked for Bass Brewers, I was part of the team that launched what I believe was Britain's first intranet. In fact, the word intranet didn't exist at that point, so it was called a Fast Electronic News Service, or FENS for short. Although it was a long time ago, many of the techniques we used to launch and embed the platform are still relevant to to-day's online communication platforms. Based on this, and more recent experience, these are my golden rules:

1. **Make sure there is a business case**
   Selling in the idea to leaders was tricky because there were no case studies or examples of best practice we could use. Our case was based on cost saving. We said that by implementing FENS, the company could stop Bass Brewers News – a printed publication that was tailored to six different regions and was posted to the homes of 20,000 employees. FENS represented a big saving in both production costs and the resource required to create it.

2. **Involve employees in design and delivery**

   Middle managers were identified as the key to
   our success. They were worried about having
   their authority undermined if their teams
   could go direct to a different source to find out
   information, and if they could find out things
   at the same time or even before their bosses.
   We involved them in the design and delivery,
   listening to their concerns and sharing benefits,
   such as pointing out that instead of simply
   reading out company announcements, they
   could have more quality conversations with
   their team members, discussing the news and its
   implications.

3. **Build capability and buy-in**

   FENS was before most people had internet at
   home and no one had it on their phones. We
   had to do a lot of training to show admins how
   to publish to FENS and employees how to find
   things on it. We also did a lot of training with
   middle managers to help them to adapt their
   communication style to suit the new platform.
   Importantly, the company made employee
   communication a mandatory and incentivised
   KPI for all middle managers, showing them
   that their role had not been replaced by a
   machine, but that it was more important than
   ever for them to have dialogue with their
   teams.

4. **Build awareness and adoption**

   People weren't used to looking on their PCs for communication, so we had to run awareness campaigns via other channels. This included a video called 'No FENS No Comment' – based on an ad for the *Financial Times* – which showed that FENS enabled employees to hear things direct from the horse's mouth and that if they weren't using it, they were missing out.

5. **Make your content sticky**

   Data showed us that the most popular two areas on FENS were the directory, which helped employees find each other's contact details, and the 'buy n' sell' site, a sort of forerunner to eBay. These were the hooks that drew people in, and while they were there, they looked at our communication.

6. **Share your successes**

   FENS became pretty famous and internal communicators from throughout the UK made the pilgrimage to Burton upon Trent to see it for themselves (or maybe just to sample the beer).

When to use print

Despite the growth in online communication, print is not dead. There is still very much a place for it in your communication strategy. Printed materials such as brochures, newsletters, postcards, flyers, letters to the home, tent cards, big pictures and posters can work well in certain circumstances, including:

- **When you want to reach non-wired workers**
  Although most communicators and their leaders sit in front of screens, it is important to remember that a large proportion of many workforces are non-wired workers. According to Google, non-wired or 'deskless' employees make up 80% of the global workforce – that's about 3 billion people. This could include frontline workers, those on production lines, in call centres or out in the field, people working in the distribution, hospitality, healthcare and retail sectors, and maintenance staff, eg in transport or utility companies. Many of these people don't have their own company phones or laptops and struggle to be in the right place, have the right logins or find the time to access shared devices. This group might also include some technophobes, who simply can't or won't engage with today's technology.

- **When you want to reach their families**
  It is sometimes useful or desirable to create communication materials that deliver messages that go beyond just employees – reaching their spouses, partners, or even kids. This is particularly true for communications about benefits or 'high concern' communications, such job changes, location changes, etc.

- **When employees like it that way**
  There are occasions when even desk-based
  employees prefer to have something in their
  hands, to peruse at their leisure. This can be
  the case when they are heavily invested in the
  content and want the opportunity to really study
  it, properly consider the information and weigh
  up the options – or if they are simply sick of
  looking at screens. A 2021 report by MetLife into
  employee benefits, for example, showed that UK
  employees rated the effectiveness of employee
  benefit handbooks and booklets as highly as
  employers' benefit websites.

- **As a follow-up or reminder**
  After a face-to-face or virtual briefing, conference
  or meeting, it can be effective to provide printed
  materials as a follow-up or reminder. This might
  include the sort of printed paper materials
  outlined above, which can be posted to homes,
  handed out, displayed in reception areas or
  canteens, or stuck on noticeboards. But they
  could even be mugs, lanyards, water bottles, etc.

Two-way communication

There is an anonymous saying that goes: 'Speak in
such a way that others love to listen to you. Listen in
such a way that others love to speak to you.' Listening
is a massively under-rated part of communication. I've already talked about its importance in the

Audience, Behaviours and Content chapters and its role in Delivery is equally vital.

Any successful relationship requires two-way communication. In the workplace, you not only share information with your employees, but you also demonstrate that you are listening to them. It's the only way you build trust. Encouraging your employees to speak up and share what they are thinking is also a great way to ensure that your communication delivery has been effective – that they have received, read and understood it and, ideally, that they are willing and able to act on it.

Many of the communication channels mentioned above are considered to be two-way, but of course, the extent of the interaction varies from comments and likes on an online platform to full dialogue and discussions in workshops, focus groups and forums. You should have a range of channels that give employees the opportunity to share their thoughts on your communication content and let them tell you how they feel about working in the company (their employee experience), to input their ideas about key topics such as customer service, quality or safety, and to voice their opinions on other aspects of the organisation, such as its vision, values and strategy.

Here are some ideas for fostering dialogue:

- Encourage leaders and managers to have regular chats or one-on-one sessions with their team members employees.

- Ensure you have a way to collect feedback from your employees, eg a dedicated email address, response forms or, for non-wired employees, postcards or comment boxes.

- Run regular polls or surveys to gather qualitative comments and quantitative data that can be compared over time.

- Ensure you have channels that allow your employees to react to messages and comment on content, and to create and share their own content.

- Encourage employees to share their ideas or best practices via a suggestion scheme.

Like all two-way communication, the most important part is not the listening itself, but what you do about what you have heard. Ideally, you will be able to take some demonstrable action, that you can report back on. But even if it turns out there is nothing you can do, you should always close the loop by telling people that and explaining why.

Encouraging online interaction

You can encourage interaction, make it easier and more fun by using some of the interaction tools that are available online. There are hundreds out there, and everyone has their favourites. Here are a few interaction tools I've come across or which have been recommended to me:

- Virtual whiteboards, eg miro.com, mural.co, jamboard.google.com

- Auto notetaker, eg otter.ai, fireflies.ai

- Leader boards, eg spinify.com, plecto.com

- Recognition, eg 15five.com, kudos.com, perkbox. com

- Team bonding, eg knowyourteam.com

- Check-ins and 1-2-1s, eg officevibe.com, cultureamp.com

- Polls and surveys, eg pollev.com, peakon.com, glintinc.com

- Mood/concept board, eg padlet.com, crello.com

- Word cloud generator, eg mentimeter.com, wordart.com

- Collaboration, eg kahootz.com, monday.com, slack.com, trello.com

Have a play with these and have a search for some more. See which you think will work best to promote interaction from and with your colleagues and then find an opportunity to give them a go.

Mastering verbal interaction

David Bradford and Carole Robin have taught interpersonal skills to MBA students at Stanford University and have also coached and consulted business executives. They share what they've learnt in their book *Connect: Building exceptional relationships with family, friends and colleagues*, in which they explain that any interaction has three parts to it, or what they call 'realities'. These are:

1. My intention or motivation (something only I know)

2. My behaviours, eg my words or tone (something we both know)

3. The intention or motivation of the other person (something only the other person knows)

Of these three realities, we can only ever know for sure about two of them, ie numbers 1 and 2. What Bradford and Robin find, however, is that in most interactions, people don't stick with what they know, they make assumptions about the other person. Problems arise when this happens, and, of course, it works both ways. They call this 'over the net', using a tennis analogy to show that when you assume that you know what is happening, you are going over the net to the other person's side, when you really should be sticking to things you know to be true, ie your own reality and feelings.

When you assume you know other people's intentions or motivations, for example, when giving feedback, a few things happen. First, the other person can get defensive and show resistance, and second, they can dispute what you are saying, so you lose power and are on the back foot. But if you say how *you* feel, you can't be told you're wrong. As such, you should focus on how the other person's behaviour makes you feel.

Watch out, though. Bradford and Robin warn that you need to make sure you are expressing what you *feel*, not what you think. If you can replace 'I feel' with 'I think' in your sentence, then it's an opinion, not a feeling, and you may be straying over the net. For example, saying, 'I feel you're not listening' takes you to the other side of the net, whereas saying, 'I don't feel heard' keeps you on your own side.

The other great thing about this technique is that it gives you and your colleagues the language with which to push back. You can say, 'I think you've gone over the net there', and it's a shorter, more subtle way to say, 'Don't assume you know what I'm thinking or why I'm doing what I'm doing.'

Summary

We've never had as many channels to choose from, but as Rachel Miller from All Things IC says, the task of a professional communicator is unchanged – it's still 'all about championing the right tools, for the right task, at the right time'. It is your role to ensure your organisation has a suite of channels that are agile, responsive and able to cater for all eventualities, and to advise on the best way to deliver a particular communication.

As we have seen, you need a broad range of communication channels to serve different purposes – to inform, connect and engage. Look back at your channel map and make sure you have got all your bases covered. This may require you to add channels into the mix, or to harvest those that are no longer fit for purpose. But beware, when deciding whether to keep or axe a communication channel, don't base your decision on user stats alone. Just because a channel only reaches a small number of people, doesn't mean it's not effective. It may be the only way for that small but important group to receive vital information.

Despite many benefits, it must be remembered that online communication is not a substitute for face-to-face or verbal communication. And don't forget that your most important communication channels, and the key to effective verbal or face-to-face communication, are your line managers and leaders. They are already in place, but there is a good chance you'll need to pay them a lot more attention and give them a lot more support than you are doing. Helping them to build their communication capability and confidence is the most effective way to improve your communication delivery, so if you do nothing else, do that.

Musing 5: Glastonbury – how do you make people feel?

Like many mourning festival fans, we had a #Glasthomebury in our garden in 2020 and 2021. Small groups of socially distanced friends joined us over a few days to eat, drink and be merry – with music. It got me thinking about why the real-life Glastonbury experience is so special. The line-up varies, the weather can be atrocious, the facilities are primitive, and yet it's one of the hottest tickets on earth.

Maybe it's because of the F-word – how it makes you feel, such as:

- Valued: The organisers don't take their festival-goers for granted and are always looking for ways to make the experience even better.
- Trusted: Of course, there are some parameters, but within these you're free to be yourself.
- Part of a tribe: You know that everyone around you shares broadly the same values and they are there for much the same purpose.

As internal communicators, as well as inputs – ie what we're telling people – we should also be focusing on outcomes – ie how we're making them feel. If employees feel valued, trusted and part of your tribe, they're very likely to stay with you, strive for you and sing your praises.

6
Evaluation

As we discussed in the previous chapter, sending stuff out is easy. Communicators have never had so many channels through which to deliver their content. But don't be caught out by the 'communication illusion' – the belief that if something has been sent out, it has been communicated. Communication only really happens when your content has been received, understood and acted on. Until then, it's just information.

Another mistake is assuming you know what people are thinking. Don't assume, ask. Then listen to what they say, understand it and act on it. These are the three vital parts of evaluation: Ask – Analyse – Act. It always amazes me how much time, money and effort some organisations spend on doing the first part, without really delivering on the second two.

So, once you've established exactly **who** your communication is aimed at (Audiences), **why** you are communicating with them (Behaviours), **what** you are communicating (Content) and **how** to communicate (Delivery), the final set of questions to ask are about evaluation, ie:

- What does success look like? How will you know if your communication has achieved its objectives?

- What measures do you need? Before and after? Inputs or outputs? Qualitative or quantitative?

- What next? How will you demonstrate that you've listened to and acted on the results?

What to evaluate

The good news is that using the ABCDE model makes the evaluation stage straightforward. This is because, by completing the previous stages, you already know exactly who and what you need to measure to see if your communication has achieved its objectives.

But you still need to be careful to make sure you're applying the right measures. For example, if retention was one of your measures and it was scoring highly, you may think you're doing well. However, it might be that people are staying for the wrong reasons, eg because they've got nowhere else to go. If they aren't engaged, then their continued presence could be doing more harm than good. Going back to the SMART model, you may need to be more specific about what you mean by retention, defining exactly who you want to keep and then measuring against that.

Another thing to watch out for is to make sure you're focusing on measuring outcomes as well as inputs. Just tallying numbers doesn't count. What really matters is the action that's taken as a result of the communication, not how many hits or likes your post got, or how many people attended your event. Going back to the ICE model in Chapter 3, you are trying to find out if, as a result of your communication, your audience is more informed, connected or engaged.

Ideally, when deciding what you are evaluating, you will need a mix of both quantitative and qualitative measures. Let's look at each of these in turn.

Quantitative measures

Quantitative measures provide you with data. They tell you about what, who and when, which is great for understanding what is going on and learning from it.

The danger, particularly with digital platforms, is that everything is measured, so we're absolutely deluged with data. Figures aren't always a communicator's natural stomping ground, but it is important that you really get to grips with what they're telling you. Think of it like *Dragon's Den*, where you always need to know your numbers.

Data is your friend. Make a habit of looking at it, analysing it and learning from it. It will tell you which days and times work best for different audiences, which links, which formats, which senders, etc. You can use this to fine-tune what you send, when you send it and who you send it from. It also demonstrates what works and what doesn't. If someone is asking you to issue something in a way that you know won't work, you can make an alternative suggestion and use the data to back this up.

But don't forget, in the words of William Bruce Cameron, not everything that can be counted counts, and not everything that counts can be counted.

Qualitative measures

Qualitative measures provide you with information based on opinions and experiences. They tell you about how and why, which is also great for understanding what is going on and learning from it.

If you want to know if your audience received your communication, you should use quantitative methods. If you want to know if they understood it and if it changed their mindset or behaviour, you need to use qualitative methods. This will complement your data, making it more compelling and adding richness through comments and stories.

Using both methods together will demonstrate the ability of communication not just to inform, but to connect people and, ultimately, to engage them so they change their behaviours.

 ## Standards for measuring internal communication

A study aimed at developing standards for measuring internal communication conducted by the Institute of Public Relations and the Commission on Research, Measurement & Evaluation and published in 2018 defined twenty-two standards across three categories – out-takes, outcomes and organisational impact.

Measuring **out-takes** includes seeing whether employees' awareness, knowledge or understanding have changed; how relevant the communication was; and how much information they retained.

Measuring **outcomes** focuses more on evaluating changes in employees' attitudes or behaviours. This could include their levels of advocacy, collaboration, teamwork, discretionary effort, trust and satisfaction. You may also want to gauge what they think about the organisation's authenticity, transparency and fairness, as well as how empowered they feel. Although it is not mentioned in the study, psychological safety is another important outcome that could be measured.

Measuring **organisational impact** concentrates on factors that affect the business performance, such as productivity, innovation, continuous improvement and safety. It could also include employee retention and the internal and external reputation of the organisation.

Of course, you don't have to use all of these every time you want to measure your internal communication, but they provide a useful checklist to help you decide exactly what it is you are evaluating. And, because objectives and measurement are so closely linked, you could also use these standards to guide your objective-setting at the Behaviours stage of your communication planning.

Evaluation methods

Evaluation doesn't have to be a massive set piece, like an annual engagement survey or a full-blown internal communication audit, although these can be valuable and effective if the results are really understood and acted on. There's a range of evaluation tools you can use. The key is to make sure you build some sort of measurement into every communication you do, not just to see if it's working from a communication point of view, but to see if it's delivering against business strategy too. This will provide you with data and information that will either show you that what you're doing is having a valuable impact – or that it isn't, which is just as important to know. As the Chartered Institute of Public Relations (CIPR) and Institute of Internal Communication (IoIC) 2019 *Research Report* put it: 'The key is really all about our attitude and willingness to understand and apply the tools available. As practitioners we need to proactively approach measurement from the perspective of the strategy and clear objectives.'

Below, I'll explore some of the most frequently used methods for evaluating internal communication.

Data

Start with what you've got, which is probably lots of internal communication data about who is looking at what, where and when. Analysing this will help you to understand and refine your communication content, delivery and scheduling, but keep in mind that this sort of data won't tell you whether your communication is resulting in a change in awareness, understanding, buy-in or behaviour.

The other data to find and track is company performance data. Look back at the standards in the previous section and see how many of them are already measured on an ongoing basis by other departments.

This is especially true of the organisational impact section, eg productivity, innovation, reputation, employee retention and safety. To these, I'd also add financial and marketplace performance. Anything that is important to your organisation will be measured, and if something is important enough to be measured, your internal communication activities should be having a positive impact on those figures.

Instant response

A quick and dirty way to measure communication effectiveness is through instant-response mechanisms, such as polls, voting, word clouds, etc. Although these methods work particularly well online, you can achieve the same effect 'in real life' if you're looking for instant responses from non-wired workers. For instance, you could do some vox pops, or you could ask them to tick items on a list, put stickers, smiley faces or traffic lights on statements they agree/disagree with, or drop ping pong balls or counters into different boxes or slots.

Sometimes that's all you need, just a quick check-in to show that what you're doing is hitting the mark – or not.

Surveys

However, if you want to gather input more formally and from lots of people then you're probably going to need to use some sort of survey. It's actually pretty simple – decide what you want to know and from whom, design some questions, ask the right people and see what they say. Of course, there's more to it than that, but that is the basic premise.

Surveys can range from short, frequent pulse surveys to in-depth, annual engagement surveys. You can design and run them yourself using an online tool such as Survey Monkey, or you can buy in the whole process from a specialist supplier such as Gallup or Glint.

Whichever way you decide to approach a survey, you need to plan and execute it well. Here are some tips and techniques to boost the chances of your survey succeeding:

- **Determine what you want to know from the survey.** For measuring communication effectiveness, make sure this links directly to your communication objectives.

- **Decide on the type of survey,** eg Pulse or Annual Survey? Online, face-to-face, print or a mix?

- **Design your questions.** Keep each question short and make sure it is clear what you're asking – don't combine two questions into one, eg 'Does your manager communicate well and frequently?' Also, keep the number of questions to a minimum. People are busy. Respect their time and only ask them questions if you know you will be able to act on their responses.

- **Decide whether your survey will be confidential or anonymous.** Trust is key to your survey's success. Potential respondents need to know that their identities won't be revealed (at least not without their permission).

For this last point, there are different implications for you and your respondents, depending on whether you choose anonymity or confidentiality. When data is collected and held anonymously, there is no way to link the information to the respondent and not even the researcher could identify a specific participant. Online surveys can usually be conducted anonymously, as long as the IP addresses of the respondents are not stored. When data is collected and held confidentially, the researcher can identify the respondents, for example because they assign a number or code to individuals or because it was a face-to-face or telephone survey.

Whichever you choose, you need to make sure that demographic and other questions don't inadvertently reveal who individual respondents are. For this reason, reports are not usually provided for groups of five or fewer, as small groups make it easier to identify individuals. Of course, you also need to make sure you are complying with GDPR.

Now that you have designed your survey, you need to encourage responses. Here are some ideas that will help you to maximise participation:

- Tell your audience the purpose of the survey and why their responses are important.

- Respect their time. Keep the survey simple, short and relevant.

- Make sure it works well across multiple channels, eg PCs, mobiles, etc.

- Think about hard-to-reach employees. Do you need to provide translations or printed copies? Should you arrange to have access to shared PCs? Does down time need to be allocated for completion of the survey (eg for call centres or factory workers)?

- Brand it and promote it frequently across all your communication channels.

- Get leadership and line manager buy-in to ensure they encourage their teams to respond, and give them the time and space to do so. But avoid any sort of cross-departmental competition about response rates, as I've found this can lead to the wrong behaviours and leave an impression that it's all about the numbers, rather than about listening to what is actually being said.

- Have a realistic time window for completion
  – too short and it won't take account of shifts,
  holidays, etc. Too long and it may get put off or
  forgotten about.

- Offer an incentive, such as a voucher or a
  donation to the company charity, but bear in
  mind this might compromise confidentiality, as
  respondents will need to provide their contact
  details to receive the incentive.

- Say thank you at the end of the survey.

- Tell them what will happen next – and then make
  sure it does.

After the survey, it is vital to listen to, learn from and
act on the results. I've often heard leaders try to explain away or bury findings they don't like, with comments like, 'They're bound to say that, aren't they?'
Ignoring what employees have told you doesn't make
it go away, but it does undermine trust and damage
engagement.

You must always share the findings with employees,
acknowledge what they have told you and tell them
what is happening next, making sure you manage
their expectations. Don't give the impression that the
people on high will fix everything they aren't happy
with just because they've voiced their concerns. Be
clear about what will be addressed top-down – usually company-wide issues – and what will be addressed
bottom-up – usually team or local issues. If there's

something you know can't be addressed, eg pay rates, then don't ask the questions. If you've asked a question and got their responses but no action is being taken on a particular issue, make sure you tell them that and explain why.

Link your ongoing internal communication back to your survey results, not just in an immediate 'You said, we did' way, but whenever you're announcing something that they gave you their opinion on. The more you do this, the more likely they are to complete future surveys and see them as a valuable feedback tool.

Interviews and focus groups

Interviews and focus groups are great when your sample group is small. They involve asking your questions to one person (interview) or a group of people (focus group) then seeking to find themes, or indeed differences, across the different discussions. Because they're conducted in person, either face-to-face, online or via the telephone, they provide an opportunity for interaction, enabling the questioner to explore answers, ask follow-up questions and clarify understanding.

Interviews and focus groups can also be used as a precursor to a survey, helping you to shape the right topics and questions. They can also be used as a follow-up measure, helping you to understand the responses received and to explore solutions.

Workplace forums

Workplace forums are a bit like focus groups, but they are more formal and tend to be used on an ongoing basis for employers to share their ideas with and hear the views and concerns of elected employee representatives. They also provide useful opportunities for employees to share their ideas with leaders and ask them questions.

The workplace relationship service Acas believes that a workplace forum is a good way to:

- Build trust between employees and their employer

- Test ideas and seek feedback in a safe setting

- Enhance employee engagement, leading to better performance and productivity

- Improve staff wellbeing and reduce workplace stress

- Encourage greater involvement and speedier decision-making

- Reduce the likelihood of disagreements happening later

Although workplace forums are often HR-led, they are useful from an internal communication point of view as they give access to direct feedback from employee representatives and can be used to elicit their input into and/or their opinion about, either ongoing internal communication or one-off campaigns.

Employee Resource Groups (ERGs)

Also known as affinity groups or business network groups, these are employees who join together to support one another in their workplace. They have traditionally been based around shared characteristics or life experiences such as disability, sexual orientation, gender, race, age, etc, but they can also focus on interest-based topics such as the environment, charity and community and workplace wellness.

When measuring the effectiveness of internal communication, it is useful to get input from ERGs, to make sure these special interest groups are being reached and that any particular considerations they have are being taken into account.

Communication panels/champions

Alongside ERGs, you may wish to set up specialist communication panels or champions to focus on a particular aspect of your internal communication. This might be an editorial panel, to contribute to or critique your communication content, or communication champions at a site or department level, to deliver your communication and gather feedback on your behalf. Generally, these will be volunteers who are keen to help because they have a special interest in or enthusiasm for communication. As such, they provide useful eyes and ears on the ground, and often give you an unfiltered view of what's working, what isn't and what's missing.

Observation

Sometimes you just can't beat seeing for yourself what is actually happening. For example, does anyone look at the noticeboards next to the canteen, or are they too busy queueing for their food? Perhaps the food queue blocks access to the noticeboards, so people can't see what is on there even if they wanted to. Get yourself out there, look, listen and learn. It'll always be time well spent.

Potential pitfalls

Benchmarking

Leaders and line managers are always interested in how they're doing compared to others, but beware of benchmarking. External benchmarking can be misleading. If you tried to copy a competitor's evaluation method, for example, the questions would need to be exactly the same, but even then, the context would be different. Different organisations, even in the same sector, have different strategies and structures and are at different stages in their lifecycles.

Similarly, even benchmarking your internal communication impact internally across departments is pretty meaningless, unless you can show that all other factors are equal, ie content, channels and capability. Again, even then, each department has its own challenges and special circumstances that may affect the results.

The most useful thing to benchmark against is yourself, over time. That shows if you're improving or going backwards.

Sample size

The whole group of people you want to collect information from is called the population. A census aims to gather information about every individual in your population. A survey gathers information from a part of your population that you believe to represent the whole. To be 100% sure that your responses are fully representative of the audience you are measuring, you'd really need to do a census – that is, include and get a response from everyone in your population. However, that is not often practical, or even necessary, so it's more usual to do a survey to seek feedback from a representative sample of your population. But how do you know what sample size is representative?

Survey Monkey has a formula to calculate how many people you need to send your survey to. It includes questions about your population, how accurate you need to be, what sample size you need and how responsive your people are likely to be. You can find this at www.surveymonkey.com/mp/sample-size.

Response rate

With internal communication surveys, you're likely to send them out to the whole of your population, and what you are most interested in is getting a good response rate that you're confident is representative of your audience.

Employee feedback platform Hive call this your 'authentic response rate'. They believe this data 'will be packed with real insights that are a true reflection of how people are feeling – aka authentic responses – and that's way more important than focusing on response rate numbers alone'. They recommend response-rate goals of over 70% for your engagement surveys and over 50% for your pulse surveys.

Frequency

How often should you measure your internal communication? The answer is *all the time*. Obviously, you can't ask the same employees the same questions over and over again, but you can and should put measures in place for every piece of communication you do.

Use evaluation as a tool, not a weapon

And finally, make sure you and those around you use the results of your internal communication evaluation as a tool to help focus on continuous improvement and not as a weapon to beat people with.

Auditing internal communication

The aim of an internal communication audit is usually to understand the effectiveness of your current internal communication strategy and identify opportunities for improvement. I've undertaken independent, impartial internal communications audits for many large and medium-sized organisations in the private and public sectors. In doing so, I have tended to focus on reviewing their existing internal communication across three key aspects to ensure that these are fit for purpose. These are:

- **Content** – Does your internal communication tell a clear, concise and compelling story?

- **Channels** – Do you have the right mix of one- and two-way channels including face-to-face, print, online and social?

- **Capability** – Do your leaders and line managers understand the importance of internal communication and are they willing and able to play their part in delivering it?

Planning an internal communication audit

On her 'All Things IC' blog, Rachel Miller lists the things to think through when planning an internal communication audit. I have shared and built on these here:

1. **Purpose:** Why are you auditing your internal communication?

2. **Scope:** What will be included (eg channels, content, capability)?

3. **Method:** Primary or secondary research? Qualitative or quantitative research?

4. **Timing:** How long will it take?

5. **Frequency:** Will you repeat it every month/six months/year?

6. **Resources:** Do your aspirations match your available time and budget?

7. **Impartiality:** Can your in-house communication team analyse the insights objectively or do you need to outsource this to a third-party?

8. **Representation:** Are all in-scope functions, roles, levels and locations represented?

9. **Pre-communication:** Have you told people you're doing it?

10. **Results and recommendations:** What will I act on now/next/never?

11. **Post-communication:** Have you shared the results and timeline for any actions?

12. **Evaluation:** Did you achieve what you set out to? Have you captured lessons learnt for next time?

How you undertake your internal communication audit will depend on the answers to these questions, but whatever you decide, you can use a blend of any of the evaluation methods listed above to help you achieve your purpose.

Summary

If you want to get buy-in from leaders and a seat at the top table, you need to take evaluation seriously and use it to demonstrate the value you are adding to the things that really matter to the business, and ultimately, to the bottom line. Bill Quirke is clear on the benefits of evaluation: 'Measurement helps replace opinion with fact, tracks progress towards objectives and changes behaviour by focusing people's attention on what they need to do differently... [It] helps internal communicators to demonstrate they are providing value in a language that the business understands.'

Don't be put off by the numbers or put evaluation into the too-difficult box and don't move on to the next activity without first evaluating what you've already done. This will not only earn you the respect of your top team, but it is also an essential ingredient in any internal communication award entry – and award wins are, in themselves, a great form of evaluation, especially as they're independently judged against your internal communication industry peers.

First, make sure you are very clear on the purpose of your communication. That way you will know what you are evaluating against. To do that answer the questions set out at the beginning of the chapter about what success looks like for you, and how you will know if your communication has achieved its objectives. Next, decide on how to undertake your evaluation. Finally, and most importantly, ask yourself how you'll show you have listened to, understood and acted on the results.

A useful by-product of evaluation is that it enables you to identify internal communication activities that aren't meeting their objectives and stop doing them. That means you can focus on doing less, but doing it better.

The value of evaluation is clear, and your options are many, so what are you waiting for? Get measuring.

 Adding Value Exercise

Ask yourself the following questions:

1. **What are the key value drivers for your organisation?**

   What do your leaders consider to be most important, what do they talk about most, what do they measure most? What issues (challenges or opportunities) are keeping your CEO awake at night?

2. **What are you as an internal communication professional doing to add value in these areas?**

   How is internal communication adding value? What more could you do? Are you spending time doing things that don't add value? How can you stop or do less of these?

3. **How are you demonstrating that what you are doing is adding real value?**

   What evidence do you have to prove what impact your contribution is having/could have? What more could you do to prove that what you do positively impacts the things that matter to your organisation?

Musing 6:
Joy Division – Atmosphere

It's now over forty years since the death by suicide of Ian Curtis, the twenty-three-year-old front man of cult band Joy Division. Curtis was suffering from depression and epilepsy, as well as struggling with a failing marriage, fatherhood and emerging fame. In this context, the lyrics of the song 'Atmosphere' take on even more poignant a meaning.

His former band mates say they feel guilty they didn't realise how much he was suffering. But in those days, mental health wasn't something that was talked about, especially by young men.

Thinking back to my younger days, I can now see that people I was close to were having problems, but at the time I didn't have the understanding, the vocabulary or probably the courage to have those conversations. Thankfully, awareness and understanding have increased massively in recent years and there's lots of useful advice online.

Much of it comes down to communication. Ask people how they are feeling, then really listen to what they say – and what they don't say. And if you're not feeling great, please tell someone and let them help. Be kind to yourself and others.

7

& Beyond

There are some things you'll need to consider in your internal communication planning and delivery that aren't included in the ABCDE model. I usually extend the model to include F for Funding and G for Good timing, and beyond that there are some other important considerations. These are covered in this chapter.

Funding

Money matters. Whether you are in-house, a consultant or freelance, your internal communication activities need to be funded somehow. There are two major areas of cost related to delivering internal communication. The first is the cost to your organisation or client of having you and your team on board. This includes the direct cost of employing you – your fees, wages, expenses, national insurance, pension, work benefits, and that of managing and developing you. Even if you're a volunteer, there will be some cost involved, such as that of time spent by others managing and training you.

The second area of cost is what I call your 'spending money'. These are the things that are delivered by some sort of supplier, which you will be invoiced for. The supplier could be an agency, consultant or freelancer that is providing you with extra resource and expertise to help you with understanding your audiences, defining your desired behaviours, creating your content, developing your delivery or evaluating your success. Or it could be a supplier that is providing you with some sort of product or service that helps you to deliver those things, from top-end technology such as an internal communication platform or tool, to printed publications and materials, events or activities, the latest lanyards or team T-shirts, or even commemorative cupcakes.

The important thing is to make sure that all these costs are seen as value-adding. You want your organisation to see any expenditure as a valuable investment in your skills and abilities and, most importantly, in what you are delivering to the bottom line. In other words, ask not what your organisation can do for you, but tell them what you are doing for them.

In Chapter 1, I talked about the value of communication. What you do builds employee trust and engagement, it improves organisational culture, and it increases productivity. Keep reminding your leaders of this. Don't wait to be asked. Make sure you regularly report on your achievements and do it in a language that they understand – the language of money, or, as marketing guru Chris Bevolo says: 'Financial – money – dough – bottom line – coin – or, as I like to call it, ROI.'

Bevolo defines Return on Investment (ROI) as 'the net financial revenue to the organisation from the effort, after having accounted for the effort's cost.'

There is a simple formula for this:

$$ROI = \frac{(\text{financial gain or saving} - \text{cost})}{\text{cost}}$$

You don't need any special technology and you don't need to be particularly good at maths, you just need to be able to show that the benefit of what you're doing is more than the cost. And actually, if it turns out that it isn't, then that's useful information too, because it gives you the evidence you need to stop and try something different instead.

Look back at Chapter 6 and make sure that you're using a combination of the evaluation techniques outlined there to provide quantitative and qualitative proof that you and your activities are money well spent.

It's one thing to justify the cost of what is being spent on internal communication, but the other key aspects of funding are getting hold of it in the first place and then managing what you've got.

Whether you're in-house or in an agency, there will be an annual budgeting process and it's vital that you get to grips with this. Your organisation has finite funds to distribute across all its functions, and you need to make sure you're getting your fair share. To do this, you must justify what you're asking for by demonstrating value and ROI, but you should also know the system. This is where the finance manager is your friend.

First, you need to know the budget cycle, ie the period it covers, when your forecast is required and when budget approval takes place. You'll also need to know the correct procedure at the end of the budget cycle, eg when and how to accrue for items that have happened but haven't yet been invoiced.

Then you need to construct your forecast. Figure out everything you're going to spend – both people costs and spending money – and make sure you include them. At this stage, you'll probably also need to allocate your costs across the duration of the budget, eg twelve months or thirteen periods, or however your organisation splits its financial year. Where you know when a cost is going to be incurred, eg an annual event or survey, allocate the amount to that time period. Otherwise, make an educated guess as to when the money will be spent, or spread the cost equally over the time periods.

Don't hold back. Put everything into your forecast, because if it doesn't go in now, you might have to wait a full year for another chance. It's much more difficult to get funding allocated outside of the official budgeting cycle, which is why being strategic and thinking well ahead are vital. You might not get approval for everything you ask for, but at least you'll have given it a go. On that point, it's also important to prioritise. What are the must-have items vs the nice-to-have items and why? That way, if/when you get asked to revise your budget (usually downwards), you'll know which items you're willing to sacrifice and which you're willing to fight for, and be able to justify your case.

Once you have your budget, you need to keep on top of it. Review it regularly and make sure everything you're spending is being accounted for. Finance folks hate surprises, so if something changes, whether it's how much you're being invoiced or when, let them know. The most important thing to keep your eye on is the bottom right-hand corner, ie the total spend. If you overspend on one activity or in one time period, make sure you underspend elsewhere to even things out.

Think of it like your household expenses and balance your books. Being seen as mature with money will enhance your reputation. It's unlikely anyone will pat you on the back or praise you for getting it right, but you can guarantee someone will let you know about it if you get it wrong.

Good timing

There are three considerations when it comes to timing your communication. First, there's the timing of when you should get involved in any conversation that is ultimately going to require your support. Generally speaking, the earlier you are involved, the better the results. Being part of the discussion from an early stage enables you to shape not just the communication, but the overall plan. You will also be able to use your unique knowledge of other things going on across the organisation – which those on the project team may not have – to provide some valuable air traffic control.

But beware. Being involved early is one thing, but sitting through hours of detailed project management meetings is potentially not the best use of your time. Try to ensure that internal communication is on the agenda for every meeting, but that you are not the only person responsible or accountable for it. That way, someone else on the project team will have it on their radar and can call you in for your specific expertise and guidance only when it is needed.

The second aspect of timing to consider is when to communicate. There are some philosophical considerations here, for example about what stage in a project you start to talk about it with your internal audiences. Of course, the answer may be different for different audiences, but you need to agree some general principles with the project or leadership team.

I find it helpful to get them to think of this like a cake. Do they want to wait till it is fully baked to tell people about it, or do they start telling them about the ingredients, the recipe, what it's going to look and taste like, before they even have the full cake? Although the answers will vary depending on what you are communicating, having the conversation in this way will help you to understand their thinking and advise them accordingly.

There are also some practical considerations to take into account. For example, if you're making a major announcement that needs to reach everyone at the same time, you will have to consider things like shift workers, global time zones and the ability of your audience to access your channels of communication, and, if announcements are being made via leaders or line managers, then exactly who is saying what, when and to whom. Major announcements often require a highly choreographed timetable to ensure that audiences hear the right messages from the right person at the right time.

Even then, your best endeavours might be thwarted by matters beyond your control. For example, for listed companies, commercially sensitive announcements will need to be made to the stock exchange first. This usually happens as soon as the relevant stock exchange opens. The London Stock Exchange opens at 8am, for example. As soon as any stock exchange announcement is made, it is in the public domain and you're playing catch-up with your internal communication to ensure your employees hear the news from the company and not from the media, especially if it affects them personally. Another risk outside of your control is a leak to the media. This could come from anywhere at any time, so it's always wise to have a reactive statement at the ready and to be prepared to adjust your timetable if the cat gets out of the bag.

The third timing-related consideration is the rhythm of your internal communication, the day-to-day drumbeat. Your internal communication calendar should include all the regular announcements, briefings and events, such as daily updates, weekly round-ups, monthly leadership briefings, quarterly away days, annual conferences, etc. This not only allows you to see at a glance all the opportunities you have to get internal communication content out to (and from) various audiences, but it also enables some valuable air traffic control, so you can avoid audience overload. It will also help you to spot – and rectify – any gaps or overlaps and, importantly, to manage audience expectations. For example, if it's Friday, they might know to look out for the weekly roundup. If it's the first Wednesday of the month, they might expect a leadership briefing. By creating a regular rhythm in this way, your internal communication programme will appear more professional and planned and your audience can ensure their other appointments are scheduled around these recurring calendar items.

In business, if you want something to happen, you've got to structure it in. So always make sure you have all your major internal communication milestones in your calendar well in advance. All your stakeholders should have these key dates in their diaries too – this includes the leaders and line managers, as well the relevant audiences.

Crisis communication

No matter how well you have planned your internal communication calendar, things can get thrown off course by an unexpected event or even a crisis. Unfortunately, that's something we all became very familiar with when the coronavirus pandemic hit in 2020. Some organisations were better placed to respond than others and that showed both in their internal communication response and in the magnitude of the subsequent impact on their reputation.

I've always thought the term 'crisis planning' is a bit of an oxymoron. After all, none of us could really claim to have planned for the coronavirus crisis hitting. I prefer to think of it as 'crisis preparedness'. The author and entrepreneur Margaret Heffernan agrees. Speaking on *The Spark* on BBC Radio Four, she said, 'We have an appetite for certainty, but we shouldn't feel the need to feed it. Instead, ask yourself, if this happened, what would you wish you had in place?'

In their eBook *Communicating in Crisis*, intranet software company Interact suggest seven steps that will help you prepare for an unexpected scenario. I have shared and built on these here:

1. **Anticipate eventualities**
   Brainstorm scenarios – ideally with a mix of leaders, managers and frontline workers. Regularly scan the horizon for early warning of potential issues or events that may become crises.

2. **Create a crisis team**
   In a crisis, leaders will usually call on their HR, legal and communication leads, as well as any relevant subject matter experts. Make sure that all contact details are shared and that everyone knows who is doing what and can easily get hold of one another. Minimise bottlenecks by ensuring decision-making authority is pushed down to the right levels. At crisis point, those at the very top are likely to be busy being the company spokespeople or solving the most significant or strategically critical problems.

3. **Know your audiences**

   The better you know your audiences, the more effectively you will be able to communicate with them when a crisis hits. This is where the personas we looked at in Chapter 2 can come in handy, helping you to group different types of employees and decide how best to reach them or hear from them.

4. **Map your channels**

   You're probably going to need to use every one of them, so make sure they're working efficiently and that you have up-to-date information about the necessary permissions, rights and access. Ideally, you should be able to monitor not just what has gone out, but what has been received.

5. **Make sure they're two-way**

   Check you have channels in place that can receive communication as well as broadcast it. Your employees can be a great source of on-the-ground information and ideas, and you need them to be able to get those to you quickly and easily.

6. **Check your policies and procedures**

   Make sure they're up-to-date and easily accessible. It's best to do this regularly, so that they're ready to refer to or follow in a crisis.

7. Prepare some holding statements and templates
You may not know what crisis is going to hit or when, but you can get a head start, by having some generic holding statements and templates in place, ready for modification and quick release as and when needed.

Interact concludes with the warning that employees 'can be our greatest asset, or potentially, our biggest liability… Failing to plan and prepare them effectively will incur further damage, threatens your brand reputation and in serious cases, may even pose a threat to the very existence of your organisation.'

 Crisis Preparation Exercise

It's an easy thing to put off, but I suggest that you block out some time in your calendar over the next two weeks to do the following:

1. Identify those people in your organisation who will play key roles in a crisis situation.
2. Schedule some time with them to brainstorm scenarios, anticipate eventualities and get some early warning systems in place.

Then, in the two weeks after that:

3. Review steps two to seven in the list of ways to prepare in the above section. Most of these are things you can be getting on with yourself.

4. Do as much as you can, then take what you've done back to the group to get their input, buy-in and sign-off.

5. Schedule regular check-ins so that when a crisis hits, you're as prepared as you can be.

Not every issue becomes a crisis and in fact, the correct early response can help minimise the damage and even turn a challenge into an opportunity to positively reinforce your organisation's reputation.

When I was working in public relations, I came across a great model for damage limitation that I have used ever since. It can be applied to many situations, both for internal and external communication and even outside of the workplace. These are the Three Rs – Regret, Reason and Remedy. Broadcaster and media trainer Bill McFarlan advises applying the Three Rs when something goes wrong.

 The Three Rs model

- **Regret** – First, say you're sorry for what has happened or for how people are feeling. Lawyers don't always like this, seeing an apology as a potential admission of liability, but if you work with them, you should be able to come up with a form of words that satisfies both legal and communication requirements. And, as McFarlan points out, sometimes simply saying sorry at the earliest opportunity can actually prevent subsequent legal action.

- **Reason** – The next thing to do is offer an explanation. Tell people why the situation occurred or what you're doing to find that out.

- **Remedy** – Finally, share a solution. Tell them what you're doing to prevent it ever happening again. This must be sincere. Once you've said it, it's important you do everything you can to prevent reoccurrence.

Here is a perfect example of getting this wrong and then getting it right, both from the same company.

A well-known company, which prides itself on its people-first values, had an issue when some former employees issued an open letter on Twitter complaining of a 'toxic working environment'.

The initial response from the company implied that those who had written the letter simply weren't suited to their fast-paced environment. This outraged the original letter writers and fuelled another tweet, in which they said it was 'grotesque' to suggest that staff who voiced concerns were underperforming or simply could not hack the pace.

Eventually, the company got it right, issuing a follow-up statement which addressed the Three Rs:

> 'As a fast-growing business **[reason]**, we have always tried to do the best by our team… We are going to reach out to our entire team past and present to learn more **[remedy]**. But most of all, right now, we are sorry **[regret]**.'

If only they'd said that first time around, they'd have avoided another day of negative headlines and crisis communication inside and outside of the company.

After a crisis

Once a crisis has been averted, leaders can stop having to focus on the short-term, tactical steps they needed to take to address immediate issues, or simply to survive. Instead, they will once again be able to lift their gaze and start looking upwards (and outwards and forwards), seeking inspiration and identifying opportunities not just to survive, but to thrive.

Depending on the severity and duration of the crisis, they will need to revisit and potentially redefine their strategy. They should also reconnect with their employees, sharing the new strategy, or reinforcing the existing one, and making sure everyone is refocused

on where the company is heading and what they must
do to help it get there.

Internal communication and engagement are critical to achieving this and communicators too will be
able to lift their gaze from day-to-day firefighting and
just getting stuff out, and once more focus on adding
value to their organisations through effective strategic communication. But while doing so, don't forget
to recognise and record the learnings from the crisis.
You never know, they may come in handy for the next
time – and there will always be a next time.

Summary

By understanding and applying the ABCDE model,
along with the additional considerations we've discussed in this chapter, you've now got the knowledge
and the framework to create an internal communication strategy. This can be applied to an entire internal
communication programme or to a single project or
challenge.

That said, simply having a model and applying it
doesn't make you a strategic, value-adding internal
communicator. There's a bit more to it than that, as
you'll see in Part Three.

Musing 7: Hot Chip – tailor your content to your channel

In October 2019, I was watching Hot Chip play live at Rock City in Nottingham. I joked that I could watch them 'Over and Over' (the name of one of their songs), little realising what was to come. From March 2020, the coronavirus pandemic hit, which meant there was virtually no live music for over eighteen months.

The good news was that, during that period, some bands performed live and streamed their gigs online. This didn't always work well, but Nick Cave and Mike Skinner got the formula right. The secret of their success was that they didn't simply stand on stage and perform their set as if they were in front of a live audience. They created a show that was specifically for streaming.

Communicators can learn from these experts at engaging audiences. Don't try to replicate face-to-face formats online. Instead ask yourself what you're trying to achieve, then create channel-specific content that delivers your objectives. Or, to misquote Hot Chip's 'Over and Over', start by thinking what you want them to do. Tailor your content to your channel.

PART THREE
FAST-TRACK YOUR CAREER

What I've shared so far covers what you need to know to plan and deliver an effective internal communication strategy. Part Three covers *how* you need to operate to become, and be recognised as, a strategic internal communication professional, and by doing so, fast-track your career.

As you have learnt in Parts One and Two, an internal communicator's role is to deliver value, rather than just to do stuff. If you apply the ABCDE model to your day-to-day activities, you will be well on your way to achieving this. But if you want to fast-track your career, you should also ensure that you understand what is important to your leaders and that you are delivering, and being seen to be delivering, real added value.

When it comes to fast-tracking your career, you need to apply the same strategic rigour as you do to your internal communication planning. This is effectively a communication campaign, where the message is about you, your abilities and your ambitions. The ABCDE model is a useful starting point:

- **Audience** – Who has influence and/or control over your career? Your line manager? Members of your leadership team? Anyone else?

- **Behaviour** – What do you want them to do differently? Notice and value your work? Empower you to add more value? Promote you or give you a pay rise?

- **Content** – What key messages or content will most effectively influence your audience? Data? Success stories? Internal or external endorsements?

- **Delivery** – What opportunities do you have, or can you create, to demonstrate the value you are adding (or could add)? Involvement in projects? Ongoing programmes? Ad hoc or regular updates, eg at board meetings? Award wins?

- **Evaluation** – How will you know when you've succeeded? Promotion or pay increase? Recognition and reward? Moving onwards and upwards?

By answering these questions, you'll be thinking strategically about your internal communication career and how you can enhance it. There's more advice on this in Chapters 8 and 9.

At some points in your career, you will want to extend your thinking beyond your current role and organisation, and consider broader opportunities. What roles are open to you? What skills do you need? Who can help you? See Chapter 10 for more on this.

And last, but certainly not least, when it comes to fast-tracking your career, don't lose sight of what really matters to you as a person. Make sure you consider not simply your job title and package, but what you believe in, what you care about and what really makes you happy. We'll consider the importance of these in Chapter 11.

8
Be More Strategic

Listen to any prominent internal communicators speaking at conferences, webinars or other events, and it won't be long before you hear them discussing the need for 'senior buy-in' or 'a seat at the top table'. These seem to be perennially on the internal communicator's wish list. But rather than hoping these might magically happen, it pays to identify exactly what you need to do to be taken seriously in your organisation, or indeed, in the broader internal communication sector.

Australian internal communication expert Zora Artis believes that the four most important requirements for being taken seriously are:

- **Business acumen** – You need to understand risk, understand numbers, understand strategy and understand commercials. In short, you must understand the language of the boardroom, and what matters most to those at the top.

- **Accountability** – I talked about the importance of evaluation and measurement in Chapter 6, and I stress again, you need to be able to demonstrate that what you are delivering is adding value, not just from an internal communication perspective, but from a business-wide perspective – your activities must support your organisation's objectives.

- **Courage** – There are times when you will need to have some tough conversations with your leaders, to be their critical friend. Based on your knowledge and experience, you may need to push back on their requests and/or make alternative suggestions. I've always found that leaders respect those of us who are bold enough to challenge them and have confidence in our expertise. But unless you really think they have blind faith in your abilities, always make sure you can back up your assertions with the relevant evidence or data.

- **Curiosity** – The world of internal communication doesn't stand still. What worked yesterday may not work tomorrow, so you need to stay on top of your game. Keep up with the latest trends and innovations. Seek out inspirations and learn from connected worlds.

Strategic vs tactical communication during the pandemic

At the height of the coronavirus pandemic in 2020, it was tempting for communicators to focus on the tactics – telling people what they needed to know about Covid-19 policies and practices. Although that was important, I argued in an article in *Communicate Magazine* that it was also the communicators' role to ensure employees understood the bigger picture, so they could see why particular decisions were being made and actions taken.

As the pandemic played out, it became clear that many organisations would continue to experience less demand for their products and services while also having to put safeguards in place for their customers and colleagues. In short, a period of less income and more cost. Communicators who recognised this, talked about it, and helped colleagues adjust their expectations and behaviours accordingly, were the ones who added most value during that unique period.

My advice was, and still is, that leaders must continue to communicate about the organisation's direction and priorities, and they must also be honest about the challenges being faced, ideally seeking input and ideas to overcome these. By being more human, listening to their teams, and involving them in problem-solving, leaders build trust.

Managers also need to focus on making sure their teams have the information, equipment and conditions to do their jobs. During lockdown, they'd been forced to be more open-minded, placing more value on outputs than on inputs. The focus was on getting things done, rather than worrying too much about who was doing what, when and how. Maintaining those levels of workplace agility, flexibility and trust is key to their onward endeavours.

Trust, of course, has to be earned. Leaders and managers who had done the right thing and communicated well pre-pandemic had a head start in this. And colleagues who were seen to step up, rather than step back, were, and are more likely to be, trusted going forward too.

During the pandemic, effective internal communication helped everyone feel like they were 'in this together' and to focus on what they needed to do as individuals to ensure that their organisation not only survived but thrived. However, don't forget what Kate Jones of Tarmac said: 'We don't want to be known for great tactics – we want to be known as great value adders.'

Become a trusted advisor

It sometimes comes as a surprise to internal communicators that business leaders generally aren't that interested in internal communication as such. What they are interested in is what it can deliver for *them*. If you want to become a trusted advisor, you will need to focus your time, effort and budget on what is important to them.

Start with building an understanding of what your leaders need and want. Get to know what is keeping them awake at night. Find out what their strategy is and then figure out what they need from their people to deliver it.

As I said when we talked about behaviours in Chapter 3, your role is to help deliver the objectives of your leaders by mobilising their people. To achieve that, you must do more than just inform people or get their buy-in. What you are seeking is actual behaviour change. You need as many people as possible to be doing things differently to get a different result – one that best matches the organisation's commercial priorities.

To be a trusted advisor, it also pays to understand the tensions at the top. In my experience, the top team is not always 'top' and is not always a 'team'. Senior priorities are not necessarily aligned. The HR director will have different objectives from the IT director or the Finance director, and they may even be conflicting. The CEO's role is to get the best possible performance out of this group of individuals, and your role as an internal communication expert is to help them get the best possible performance out of their wider teams. Whether you're an in-house communicator or a consultant, it's also great if you can make them look good. If you succeed in doing this, and as long as it's not at the expense of any of their fellow leaders, you will earn their respect and be well on the way to becoming their trusted advisor.

Plan to deliver

Having identified what matters most to your leaders, and having shown that you can help them deliver on their priorities, your next step is to align all your energy towards this delivery. One way to do this is to think like a sports professional. Teams and individuals at the top of their game – athletes, footballers, rowers – make delivering look easy, but they work extremely hard to achieve their success. A key part of their on-the-day performance is how, in the time leading up to it, they set goals and then plan to deliver them.

A 2007 study by psychologist Richard Wiseman showed that 88% of people who make New Year's resolutions fail to keep them, but an extra 22% achieved their resolution when they engaged in goal-setting. Strangely, though, that statistic applied to men only. Women were more successful when they told their friends and family about their resolution, so introducing accountability to your goals can also help you achieve them.

 **Process goals**

Process goal-setting is based on having outcome, performance and process goals. This model comes from the world of sport, but it can just as easily be applied to the world of work. Breaking your goals down in this way makes it easier to organise your thinking around how you're going to actually achieve them rather than just the overall outcome.

The outcome goal is the main thing that you are working towards. It is the *why*. In sport, the outcome goal is usually about winning. While this can be motivating, achieving such a big goal may be affected by others and is therefore not fully in your control. In the sporting world, this might mean that someone outperforms you in a race or event. In the business context, your outcome goal could be to improve your company's employee engagement score. However, the actions of others within your organisation, over which you have no control, will affect the results and impact on your overall outcome.

Performance goals are the standard that you are trying to achieve. They are the *what*. Over time, performance goals build on one another to help you achieve your outcome goal. In internal communication terms, they might include establishing new channels, developing new content or building new capability.

Process goals support performance goals by giving you something to focus on as you work towards them. They are the *how*. Process goals are completely under your control. They are the small things you should focus on or do to help you achieve your performance goals. These might include introducing regular town hall meetings, offering monthly internal communication coaching sessions, or having a weekly leadership listening group.

Simply setting goals is not enough in itself. You must also make sure they are SMART, as we discussed in Chapter 3. When it comes to timings, it's better to stick to a shorter timescale like weekly, monthly or quarterly. That way, you can feel a sense of achievement as you make progress towards your overall outcome.

 Goal-setting Exercise

1. Define your overall outcome goal – the why. Ensure it is directly linked to your organisation's purpose and/or your leaders' priorities.

2. Define your performance goals – the what. Aim for a maximum of three to begin with, as each of these will have its own process goals and you don't want to get overwhelmed.

3. Define three process goals for each performance goal – the how. Make sure all these goals are SMART and have realistic timescales.

4. Think about who in your network could help you stay on track and keep you focused. Share your goals with them and ask for their support.

5. Finally, regularly review your progress. If the goals you have set yourself are truly SMART, you will be able to keep an eye on how you're doing and, like a finely tuned athlete, you will know if you're on track to win.

Know how you're spending your time

Having great goals is one thing, but having the time to deliver them is another. You can't create more hours in the day, but you can make sure you're spending the hours you have as effectively as possible. In Chapter 2, when discussing the importance of understanding your audience, I talked about undertaking a 'Day in the Life Of' or DILO exercise. These are great for providing a clear picture of where someone is spending their time, either on a daily basis (DILO) or a weekly basis (WILO). As well as applying this technique to important subsections of your audience, for example your line managers, this can be a useful tool to help you to understand where you and/or your internal communication team are spending your time. You may be surprised how much time is spent on low-level stuff that doesn't add real value.

When I was working with an in-house internal communication team at a major technology services firm, we undertook a WILO exercise. Each team member logged their activities on a daily basis over a typical week. What this revealed was that a large proportion of their time was being spent in meetings, doing admin and delivering low-level tactical communication, leaving little time for strategic, value-adding activities. This was a real eye-opener for them and gave them both the evidence to think more carefully about how they were positioning themselves and the ammunition to help them to say no to non-value-adding activities.

Learn how to say no

One of my mottos in life is say yes more than no, but when it comes to delivering your internal communication objectives, then learning to say no – nicely and effectively – is an important skill.

If you have a tendency to be a people-pleaser, and many of us communicators are, then you may find yourself staying late to create someone's charity BBQ poster or sitting through a three-hour project management meeting, where internal communication is only discussed in the 'any other business' section at the end of a seriously long agenda. Believe me, I've been there, and I've certainly worked with teams where this sort of thing is a regular occurrence.

My advice is, don't say yes just because – because you used to do it, because you can do it or because nobody else will. Only say yes if what you're saying yes to really adds value. If someone says they want a newsletter, a new channel, an event or whatever, your role is to question the need. Ask them what they are trying to achieve. Go through the ABCDE model with them. Only then can you decide whether to say yes or no – and in either case, advise them on the best way forward.

The secret to being able to say no is to have a signed-off strategy and to be clear on what your priorities are. Having a manifesto can also help with this. This formalises your role and empowers you to say no. There is no set formula for an internal communications manifesto, but don't go overboard. Try to keep it to a single page that encapsulates your *raison d'être*, which literally means your 'reason for being'.

A manifesto is not a rewrite of your strategy, but it should include any key philosophies, principles and priorities. Involve your internal communication colleagues in creating it and ideally get input and sign-off from your CEO. Then get it nicely designed and stick it on your wall (or make it your wallpaper), so that you can refer to it whenever you're deciding whether to say yes or no to a request. Share it with as many of your stakeholders as possible. Make sure they understand that you and your team are professionals, that your time is precious and finite and that it needs to be allocated wisely. Drafting and designing their charity BBQ poster is not the best use of your expertise.

Ten top tips for being more strategic

Having participated in a Poppulo virtual bootcamp in July 2020, which brought together expert internal communicators to share strategic solutions and ideas based on our wealth of experience, I recommend the following ten top tips:

1. Define and share a bold organisational purpose that people can rally around.

2. Focus on the overall employee experience, including by creating opportunities for meaningful connections.

3. Know your audience and tailor your content and channels to them – one size does not fit all.

4. Show you really care – for example about wellbeing and diversity and inclusion.

5. In a crisis, timeliness outweighs perfection – provide clarity, consistency and certainty as soon as possible.

6. Use technology as an enabler, but only if it works in sync with your people and processes.

7. Use data to inform decisions and measure effectiveness. Test new ideas quickly and kill failures fast.

8. Encourage your leaders to be authentic and help them to serve their employees, customers and communities.

9. Be a curator of conversations rather than a controller of content.

10. Inform your actions by asking curious questions and really listening to the answers.

Summary

To operate strategically, you first need to know what you are trying to achieve. This should be closely linked to your organisation's purpose and your leaders' priorities. You then need to figure out how you're going to deliver on these – plan like a sportsperson. Break down your overall goals into time-bound activities, then do them.

Consider what you and your team spend time on. Is it the right stuff? What could you stop doing that no one would notice? What could you delegate? How else could you free up time so you can focus more on strategic, value-adding deliverables?

Steve Crescenzo advocates using a three-bucket system for categorising internal communication content, but it can also be applied to prioritising your time:

1. For the stuff you shouldn't be doing, *pass*, ie just say no.

2. For the stuff you simply have to do, *publish*, ie just do it.

3. For the stuff you should be spending most of your energy on, *promote*, ie push it up your priority list.

Musing 8: Prince – Nothing Compares 2 U

The Prince album, *Sign O' The Times*, came out in 1997. Those of us who were around when it was released, Prince fans or not, will have heard these songs and, chances are, if we heard them again today, we'd still be able to sing along.

I was lucky enough to see Prince live in the 1980s, 1990s and the 2000s. He was a great performer, but it's his songs that stick. What makes them so memorable?

First, he is authentic. Prince sounds like he believes what he is saying and the lyrics really matter to him. In *Sign O' The Times*, he laments HIV, drugs, gangs, poverty, war and greed. We see what he is seeing. We share his pain.

Second, he is good at storytelling. He sets the scene, he introduces the characters, he paints a picture. We're there with him. We can see Cynthia Rose. We believe she has starfish and coffee in her lunchbox. We want to be like her.

Third, he keeps it simple and short (and indeed, 'Kiss' is another of his hits). There are thirty lines in his song 'Hot Thing' – twenty-seven of them include the words 'hot thing', sometimes more than once. We receive the message. It's repeated, it lands, it sticks. The original version of 'Hot Thing' was just over five-and-a-half minutes long. When it was remastered in 2020, it was cut to just over three-and-a-half minutes. Attention spans have shortened.

Finally, he gets noticed. He has a distinctive look, style and manner of delivery. What he is saying stands out – it cuts through.

Apply these four techniques in your internal communications, and you might just have a hit on your hands.

9

Be An Effective
Business Partner

Some organisations operate a business partnering model for internal communication. The aim of this is to integrate your role more thoroughly into business processes and to better align your day-to-day work with actual business outcomes. Even if your organisation doesn't formally operate in this way, it's useful to understand the approach so you can cherry-pick elements of it to make sure you're working closely with your internal stakeholders and adding value where it matters most to them.

Effective internal communication business partners are those who respond best to the issues and challenges of leadership and line management, which, in turn, help them to deliver better business results. As an internal communication business partner, you should be focusing on the creation and maintenance of the communication content, channels and capabilities that will best help your organisation to deliver value to its customers, colleagues, communities and, where relevant, its shareholders.

Business partner vision

The internal communication business partner vision is to be a sought-after expert and trusted advisor, who can provide useful advice and deliver effective internal communication solutions that support the business strategy. That means:

- You will be focusing on deliverables (business requirements) rather than on do-ables (internal communication activities).

- Instead of measuring process (eg how many communications are created/shared), you will be measuring results (eg the impact of your internal communication on business performance).

What good business partnering looks like

An important part of being a good internal communication business partner is your ability to advise, encourage and shape the actions and communications of the internal stakeholders (or clients) your serve. They don't know what they don't know – it's up to you to lead the conversation, ask the right questions, advise them on options and measure the outcomes to demonstrate their effectiveness (or otherwise).

As we have explored in the previous chapters, quite often what your internal stakeholders think they want and what they actually need are not the same thing. You need to use your experience and expertise to help them to define what they are really trying to achieve and then advise them on the best way to deliver that.

Business partnering mindset

Building relationships with your key stakeholders will give you the best chance of influencing them and their behaviour. This takes time. They need to see that you're on their side and delivering for them. But if you are also part of an in-house internal communication team, you will need to balance the priorities of your internal stakeholders (which may be a single team, function or region) with the broader requirements of the internal communication team, as well as the overall business.

Remember that people will be looking to you for help, so try to make sure you:

- Focus on the things that are most important to them – where you can add most value

- Use your unique position to offer a broader view of the business, to give them some perspective and some valuable air traffic control

- Give them choices, by offering a range of options rather than a single solution

- Demonstrate the value you are adding – this will help you to get or to keep your seat at the table

- Are pragmatic – recognise that you can't always get your own way, so make sure you pick your battles

Hurdles to overcome

The first hurdle is *ability*. The business partner model requires internal communication professionals to connect their work directly to the business. Not everyone can do that, or even wants to. Some internal communication professionals may never become business partners. They are stuck, and maybe even happy, in their postbox roles, delivering tactical communication and seeing little connection between what they are delivering day-to-day and the overall business results.

Others may want to step up but simply don't know how. If that is you, then spend time getting to understand the knowledge and skills that are necessary for the business partner role, then apply them.

As with most change, there is likely to be a 20–60–20 spread in abilities. The top 20% of you are probably already doing the level of work required to be a business partner. The bottom 20% will probably never get there. And, with the right training, coaching and support, the other 60% will be able to make the move.

The second hurdle is the *maturity* of the business and/or the leaders or line managers you are aligned to. Some leaders and line managers still don't fully recognise the value internal communication and engagement can bring. This could be because they have limited knowledge of the potential positive impacts that internal communication can deliver – or it could be due to past bad experiences. The only way you can really overcome this is through actions, not words. See below for some ideas on how to do this, but be warned, it won't happen overnight.

 Stepping up

The first few years of your internal communication career is about building your practical skills. These are the foundations that will enable you step up into more senior roles.

When it comes to being a successful internal communication business partner, being an internal communication subject expert is a given. The key requirements are relationship-building, negotiation skills and the ability to please multiple stakeholders with different requirements and priorities. Your role becomes more about supporting and advising and doing less of the day-to-day work.

For that, you will need gravitas, authority and nous. The main way you will gain these is through experience. This takes time, but try some of these tried-and-tested techniques to help move things forward:

- Have an internal communication strategy that starts with and supports the business strategy. It's important to remember that it's not about what the internal communicator wants to achieve but what the stakeholders want to. For example, if their business priorities are growth, quality and innovation, then make sure all your internal communications support these.

- Get your internal communication strategy signed off by your business leads – that way you can say no to things later that don't fit with the strategy. See the 'learn how to say no' section above for advice on this.

- Make sure any plan or work you deliver for a part of business (eg function or region) has clear line of sight to the business-wide plan, ie that it is joined up and part of a bigger picture. That way they can see how their bit fits in and that it is not being done in isolation.

- Identify who your real key influencers are. This might not be leaders and line managers – it could also include PAs, exec assistants, trade union officials etc. Spend time building relationships with them, find out what they value and then make sure you deliver on that.

- Make sure you can evidence that are you delivering value, not just doing tasks. To do this, you will need to demonstrate value on the terms of the person evaluating it, which may not be the same as yours.

- Avoid being pulled down into the weeds. You can be a fabulous practitioner if that is what makes you happy, but recognise that is not the same as being an effective internal communication business partner, or a trusted advisor.

- Remember that your role is to help facilitate effective internal communication across the business. Try to be an advisor, not a doer. That means you will need to delegate, prioritise and, sometimes, simply say no.

Business Partner Effectiveness Exercise

Are you being an effective business partner? Ask yourself:

1. How do you currently interact with and contract with your business leads/internal stakeholders?

2. Do you know how you are doing? If not, ask:

    *   What has been your experience of working with your internal communication business partner?

    *   In the last six months, what have you consulted with your internal communication business partner about?

    *   Rate your experience on a scale of 1 to 5. Explain your rating.

    *   What one thing could internal communication do differently to support your strategic business aims?

3. How can I build my business knowledge, eg site visits, job shadowing, sit in on meetings that aren't just about internal communication?

4. How can I create opportunities to contribute early in discussions? How can I make sure I'm adding value?

5. What are my training needs – negotiation skills, influencing, situational leadership, assertiveness?

But remember, you can't beat experience.

Summary

Even if your organisation doesn't operate a business partner model, you can still adopt elements of the approach to ensure you are offering the best support to your in-house stakeholders or clients. Working this way will help you to focus on deliverables (what the business actually requires) rather than on do-ables (internal communication activities).

Business partnering shouldn't just be thought of as a role. According to CIPD, it's both a capability and a mindset – which will help you to develop and deliver a roadmap that's aligned to and has the potential to shape the overall organisational strategy.

To be an effective internal communication business partner, you must be able to understand your audiences, define their needs, explore approaches, identify quick wins, build credibility, celebrate achievements and measure the impact of your activities. Hey, maybe a good place to start doing all of that would be with the ABCDE model?

Musing 9: Nick Cave – a masterclass in audience engagement

If you want to advise your leaders on how to engage with their audience, I suggest you get them to watch Nick Cave in concert. Even in a massive arena venue, he manages to make everyone feel engaged. Here's how:

- He lets his songs do the talking and doesn't say a lot between songs – so what he does say seems special.
- He seeks out individuals in the crowd – so everyone feels like he is singing just to them.
- He steps off the stage and mingles with the audience – so we think he is one of us.
- He invites fans to join him onstage – so we feel we can all be part of his gang.

Offstage, this connection is reinforced through an ongoing, two-way dialogue he has online with his fans He does this via a website www.theredhandfiles. com where anyone can ask him any question and he will answer it publicly and personally.

Nick Cave is not a natural leader-type, he is awkward and unusual. Over the years, he has realised that connecting with his audience is valuable. He has worked hard to get good at it and has been willing to have an open and honest dialogue with people. In short, he knows that if you want an audience to connect to you, you first have to be willing to connect to them.

10

Develop Your Career

Probably like many of you, I didn't have a yearning from an early age to be an internal communicator. In fact, I was convinced I was a PR person through and through. My first communication role was as a graduate trainee in a PR consultancy in Birmingham. I worked hard, learnt lots and rose through the ranks to become a board director. The firm was taken over by Shandwick, so before the age of thirty, I was a director of what was then the biggest PR consultancy in the world.

After taking a year out to travel, I moved in-house. I joined Bass, then Britain's biggest brewer, in external communication. I loved working on great brands like Carling, Caffrey's, Grolsch and Britain's first alcopop, Hooper's Hooch. But I soon realised that to take on the most senior in-house roles, I would need to get some internal communication experience.

I initially took on an internal communication role just to tick the box on my CV, but soon I was hooked. I realised that where external communication is like dating, internal communication, where you have a deeper, longer-term relationship with your audience, is more like a marriage. I discovered that I loved it, and I've been pursuing it with energy and enthusiasm ever since.

Energy and enthusiasm are important ingredients, but there are a few other requirements you'll need to pick up. In one of Smarp's *Great Comms Debates*, a panel of internal communication experts discussed whether being an internal communication professional was something anyone could do. They concluded that the answer was yes, as long as they had, or could acquire, the right skills. They called these the 'IC superpowers' and listed them as:

- **Co-ordination and attention to detail** – a vital and often overlooked aspect of your role

- **Active listening** – making sure you ask questions, are curious and are not afraid to challenge

- **Rapport** – you need to be able to build strong relationships and make great connections

- **Empathy** – the ability to put yourself in your audience's shoes, so you can identify with them and meet their internal communication needs

- **Storytelling** – this is less about your own writing skills and more about helping others to identify, craft and share their own stories

It's no accident that these five superpowers spell out CARES. I'd say caring about what you do, and those you do it with and for, is an important part of any internal communicator's role. After all, if you're going to spend around forty hours a week doing something, it helps if it's something you really care about.

In-house or consultancy?

A recent survey by specialist communication recruitment consultants VMA showed that internal communication skills are in high demand as it continues to be recognised more fully as a professional specialism. The survey concluded, thankfully, that 'the days when internal communications were handled by a junior HR employee with time to spare are gone.' So, with lots of opportunities out there, how do you decide which type of internal communication role is for you?

One question to ask yourself is this: do you want to work for others, for example in-house or in a consultancy, or would you prefer to work for yourself as an independent consultant, freelance, interim, or even at the head of your own agency?

I've experienced and enjoyed both. I found that working in-house gives you great depth of knowledge in your chosen field. For example, when I worked in-house for a major brewer, I was able to become a trained beer taster and be a judge at the Great British Beer Festival. I knew my stuff about beer and brewing, as well as being able to get to know important influencers in the sector and having up-to-the-minute expertise on what was happening in the brewing industry. Of course, it helps if you're interested in the product or service. I may not have appreciated my immersion in the subject quite as much if it had been something I wasn't as personally passionate about.

Working for yourself also has its advantages. It gives you great breadth of knowledge. Elsewhere in this book, I've listed all the organisations I've provided internal communication support to over the twenty years I've been specialising in it. There are over fifty of them – ranging from pharma to financial services and from manufacturing to retailing. Through these experiences, I've learnt a little about all these organisations and the sectors they are in, and I've learnt a lot about what works and what doesn't in terms of internal communication. As a result, I've been able to cross-fertilise ideas across sectors, regions and specialisms, cherry-picking and adapting approaches to suit a wide range of different circumstances. Here the passion is not so much for the particular product or project, but for the planning and delivery of a successful internal communication solution.

In both cases, what has been the most important to me is knowing that I'm making a positive difference. Just as I'm likely to be spending around forty hours a week doing my job, the employees of every organisation I've worked with are doing the same to some degree or another. I like to think that by improving internal communication, I'm making their working lives better – and that's worth getting out of bed for.

If you're feeling unsure about your next career move, I'd highly recommend reading *Why Losing Your Job Could Be the Best Thing That Ever Happened to You: Five simple steps to thrive after redundancy* by Eleanor Tweddell. You don't need to have lost your job to benefit from Eleanor's advice. She has worked in senior positions in internal communication for companies including Virgin Atlantic, Costa Coffee and Vodafone and her structured approach to thinking through your options will really help you to decide what's next for you – be that in-house, consultancy, or something completely different.

 ## Ten top tips for setting out on your own

If you're considering setting up on your own, here is some of the great advice I got from friends and colleagues when I was starting out. These tips were first published as a blog that I wrote for the interim and executive search firm re:find:

1. **Decide at the outset what type of business you want**
   Is it a lifestyle business, ie one that provides you
   with a decent income and relies solely on your
   skills, personality and efforts? Or is it one that
   can function and grow without you in it and that
   ultimately you can sell on? This will inform what
   sort of legal entity you set up and what funds
   and infrastructure you will need.

2. **Don't overcomplicate the naming and branding
   process**
   If you've established a good reputation in
   your field, use your name. Otherwise, think of
   something straightforward that is easy to spell
   and no one else is using. Get a logo designed
   (and make sure you get the IP rights to the logo
   – the designer will own them if you don't have
   them assigned in a legally binding agreement).
   Then just get yourself on Facebook, LinkedIn,
   Twitter, etc and start communicating. Having a
   great story is more important than having a great
   name or brand, so get it written and get it out
   there.

3. **However much marketing you think you'll need to
   do – you'll need to do more**
   Just because you build it, doesn't mean they'll
   come. As a start-up, you need to get yourself and
   your story out there. Tap into all your networks,
   post stories and comments on all your social

media platforms, join industry bodies, offer
to judge awards, speak at (virtual) events, etc.
Think about where your target customers are,
and make sure you're there too.

4. **When it comes to clients, you are what you eat**
Think about the types of businesses you want to
work with and target them. If your first client is
a metal basher in the Black Country, then your
subsequent clients are likely to be similar. Great,
if that's the market you're after, but don't be
scared to turn down the wrong sort of work.

5. **When it comes to prices, you can't ski uphill**
Don't undervalue yourself. See what competitors
are charging, consider what the client can afford,
think about what value you're adding and be
bold. It's better to go in high and come down,
than to try to do the opposite. Focus on the
outcomes the client is getting for their investment
(value-based, solution-selling), rather than the
inputs you're providing (day rates).

6. **Spend time working on the business as well as in it**
When you win your first client, and there's
only you in the business, it's tempting to spend
all your time and energy on them. But don't
forget that your primary focus is building your
business, not theirs. Making them happy is a
means to that end.

7. **Your first employee is a 100% increase in your headcount**

   Another key decision point is when you're too busy to look after your business and your clients on your own, you have to decide how to grow your team. If you're building a sellable business, you'll need to recruit an in-house team, people who will eventually be able to run the business without you in it. But for a lifestyle business, you may decide it's better to create a virtual team of freelancers, so you avoid ongoing overheads and can match skills exactly to client requirements.

8. **Do your housekeeping**

   It's dull but vital to keep receipts, send out your invoices, pay your suppliers, pay your taxes, pay your employees, etc. Get an expert advisor to make sure you're doing those things right. And don't forget, your clients are unlikely to pay you for at least sixty days, some as long as 120 days, so you'll need to keep a careful eye on your cashflow.

9. **Ask for help**

   People you know, and even some you don't know, will want you to succeed. They'll be keen to help you and willing to share their expertise and advice. Don't expect them to come to you though. They may think you're doing fine and don't need their help. Make sure you ask for it.

10. **Follow your heart**
     Whatever your venture is, make sure it is
     something you love and are passionate about,
     although it must of course be something that
     enough people actually want and are willing to
     pay for.

Now, the most important piece of advice: just get on
and do it!

Professional development

Whether you're setting out on your own, or pursuing
a career in-house, you'll want to complement your
on-the-job experience with some professional development. This will not only add valuable skills and
knowledge to your armoury, but will also help to el-
evate your reputation from amateur to expert.

Qualifications

A few years ago, when my daughter was applying for
universities, I went with her to the open days of six of
the top UK undergraduate degrees in media and communication. I was amazed to find that none of them
covered internal communication on their curriculum.
In these times when, according to the Edelman Trust
Barometer, businesses are the only trusted institution
and when the lines of demarcation between internal

and external communication are becoming increasing blurred, I'd have thought internal communication would be essential for anyone studying communication. But this doesn't seem to be the case, so most people joining our profession will be doing so without any specific educational qualification in it. Luckily, our professional bodies offer a range of options for studying for formal qualifications.

The CIPR, for example, offers an Internal Communication Certificate for those just getting started and an Internal Communication Diploma for more experienced practitioners. In addition, the IoIC in collaboration with Solent University, offers a Foundation Diploma, an Advanced Diploma and Masters in Internal Communication Management. At a global level, the International Association of Business Communicators (IABC) offers international equivalents that can be accessed online via the IABC Academy.

Another option is to take a broader business-based Masters, such as an MBA, and then focus your dissertation on an aspect of internal communication that interests you. This is the route I took, doing my dissertation about engaging employees following a change of ownership, a topic which has proved useful and the learning from which I have applied many times since.

Although having this sort of formal qualification is not essential to starting or progressing your internal communication career, it does show a level of commitment in terms of time and money (if you can't persuade your employer to pay for it) and will provide you with a sound foundation of theory, as well as the language and confidence to talk to your top team on their terms.

Training

Once again, our industry's professional bodies offer a wide range of training courses to support your learning and development. You don't have to be a member to participate in most of them, but I'd definitely recommend joining either the IoIC or CIPR as they will open up loads of learning and networking opportunities for you, as well as adding some credibility to your CV.

The IoIC, for example, provides professional development activity to support all six of the professional areas they've identified in their profession map. This map summarises the role internal communicators play in an organisation and describes the knowledge and skills required to fulfil that role.

Part of the IoIC's mission is to champion internal communication of the highest standard. To support this, they provide their members with numerous tools with which to plan, record and reflect on their learnings. This includes information about their Continuous Professional Development (CPD) scheme, which enables you to demonstrate your professional competence by achieving IoIC CPD Accredited Practitioner Status.

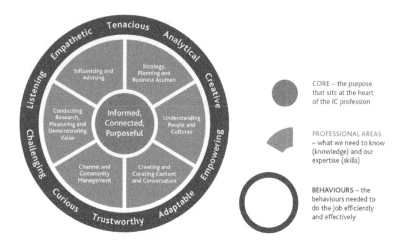

CORE – the purpose that sits at the heart of the IC profession

PROFESSIONAL AREAS – what we need to know (knowledge) and our expertise (skills)

BEHAVIOURS – the behaviours needed to do the job efficiently and effectively

The IoIC Profession Map: A framework for internal communication professionals

Similarly, CIPR run numerous training programmes and encourage their members to undertake CPD. It takes two years of continuous logging of CPD points to become an Accredited Practitioner, and you can go further and become a Chartered Practitioner.

There are lots of ways you can accumulate CPD points for either the IoIC or CIPR scheme. You can get them through formal qualifications and training, of course, but also by participating in other learning activities such as attending events and webinars, listening to podcasts, reading books and magazines or volunteering for committees and events. But remember, as CIPR points out, 'although logging points and completing CPD is important, what you learn from the activities and how you will apply them in your work is more valuable. Make sure you keep that top of mind.'

Outside of the professional bodies, there are plenty of other options for informal learning and development, many offered by practitioners and also by suppliers of internal communication platforms and services. Like many of these things, the important thing is just to get on and do some – don't sit inside your bubble, sucking on your own exhaust, get out there, see what others are doing, share best practice and learn from one another.

Influencers inside your organisation

No matter what qualifications you have or how much training you have done, a key factor in your career progression is how well you influence those around you.

We are all aware of the importance of influencers on social media, but there are also some key stakeholders within your organisation who can help you to climb the career ladder. The first person to make sure you are positively influencing is the one closest to home, ie your line manager.

Much is made of where the internal communication function sits in an organisation – is it in corporate communication or HR, does it report to the CEO or elsewhere? In many ways, it doesn't matter. I was once told by a CEO who was reducing his direct reports by moving my communication team into Group Legal that 'reporting lines are just about pay and rations, the important thing is how well you deliver for everyone on the board'. That might be a bit of a cynical view, but I have generally found it to be a helpful way of looking at it. Nevertheless, whoever your line manager is, it probably goes without saying that you need to impress them as they have the most direct influence over your progression in the organisation.

Wherever you sit in the organisation chart, you should make sure you are visible to those who matter most. That doesn't mean jumping up and down shouting, 'Look at me', but it does mean quietly and effectively offering support, adding value, pre-empting what they will need and, ideally, delivering it before they even ask you for it.

Identify your potential allies. Think about who you've helped or who needs your help (whether they know it or not). That could be senior colleagues in IT, Finance, Ops, Legal or HR, or it could be the CEO's PA. Don't do this in a cynical way – genuinely think about where you can add most value and who will benefit most from your support. Then set about collaborating with and influencing them. If, as it should be, your internal communication manifesto is linked directly to your organisation's strategy and priorities, then this should be a win–win situation. You'll be delivering against your own agenda and against theirs. Your primary aim is to do a good job, but a useful by-product of this should be that you are recognised for doing so.

Influencers in your outer networks

Obviously, influencers within your organisation are the most important if your aim is to progress your career inside that company. But if you've set your sights on moving onwards and upwards elsewhere, you'll need to build your reputation outside of your organisation too. Unlike advertising, PR or marketing, where your work is out in the public domain, there's a danger that your internal communication efforts, however great they are, will only ever seen by your employees, often sitting within firewalls or protected by commercial sensitives.

You need to find ways to shine a light on what you are doing and bring it to the attention of the influencers in the outside world. When I was Director of Communication for a major brewing company, I was based in Burton upon Trent, Staffordshire. That was definitely off the beaten path for the internal communication community, so I had to work really hard to get external recognition for the great work my team were doing. This included:

- Entering and judging industry awards

- Speaking at internal communication industry events (live and online)

- Joining the IoIC committee and running IoIC events in the Midlands region

- Networking at internal communication industry events

- Writing articles and providing comments for internal communication journals and websites

- Mentoring and sharing best practice with other practitioners

Not only did all this proactivity shine a light on what we were achieving up in Burton, but even more valuably, it also provided me with great opportunities to meet other internal communicators and learn about what they were doing. All of this benefitted me and my reputation, of course, but it was great for my team too, who saw their achievements being recognised and talked about on a par with those of other major national and international companies, often London-based. In addition, it helped build the employer brand of the company, which was perceived as a 'good place to work', not least because of its reputation for being at the leading edge of internal communication and employee engagement practices.

Summary

Your career is in your hands. No one cares about it as much as you do. It's up to you to decide what you want from your working life and then to make it happen. Energy and enthusiasm will help, but making a proactive plan and then delivering it is key.

You don't have to do this in a cynical, single-minded way. Networking, relationship-building, influencing and even formal training and development, are all two-way interactions, providing you with opportunities to both learn from others and to share your learnings.

When it comes to all these things, I've always found that the more you give, the more you get back. Be generous with your time, listen to what others have to say and share your expertise when you can. Every day is an opportunity for learning. Someone once told me to only stay in a role as long as it takes you to learn it. That might be a bit extreme, but if you're getting too comfortable and not learning anything new on a regular basis, it's time to move on.

 Career Development Exercise

It is up to you to take personal responsibility for your own career development. Don't wait for HR to contact you or for your next performance review, start your planning now. Ask yourself:

1. What is the next career move for me?
2. What skills and experience do I need to achieve this?
3. What skills and experience gaps do I have now that I need to fill?
4. How and when can I fill each of those gaps?
5. Is anything stopping me from doing those things? If so, how do I overcome those hurdles, or what is the alternative?

6. How can I build my network of influencers?

Use your answers to plan what you're going to do to in each quarter for the next year (or until you have accumulated the skills and experience you need to make your next move). Then hold yourself accountable for making it happen.

Tip: Don't just focus on training and qualifications, think more broadly about things you could do inside your organisation, like action learning, job shadowing, secondments or getting a mentor, as well as things you could do outside your organisation, such as proactively networking, joining webinars, judging panels and any other opportunities to share what you're doing and learn from others.

_____

Musing 10: The Specials – A Message to You

In my office, I've got some framed prints by graphic artist Anthony Burrill. He is renowned for posters with simple, clear messages, the best known of which is 'Work hard & be nice to people'. This is my motto as an independent communication consultant and in life in general.

My personal favourite is 'Don't say nothing', which reminds me of the lyrics of another song by The Specials, 'Do Nothing'. Like much of Burrill's work, it is open to interpretation. It could mean 'make sure you speak up', but could also mean 'make sure you don't speak up when you've got nothing to say'.

Social media makes it easy to speak up even when you've got nothing to say. It can sometimes feel like being at an awful party where everyone is standing on their own shouting about themselves. Remember the saying, often attributed to Plato, 'Wise men speak because they have something to say. Fools speak because they have to say something'.

Communication is as much about listening as speaking. It requires quality, two-way conversations. Think before you speak. Try not to be a social media shouter. Aim to have meaningful dialogues, not just loosely connected monologues. Don't say nothing.

11
Be You

As internal communicators, we are in the rare position of being able to influence not only our own fulfilment at work, but that of many others too. Through delivering effective, impactful internal communication, we have it in our power to help tens, hundreds and even thousands of people to achieve more and lead happier, healthier lives. That's a pretty inspiring thought, and even more inspiring is that the best way to do that is by being yourself.

But being yourself isn't always that easy in the workplace. First, you need to find out who you really are. If you've been in the world of work for some time, you may have lost sight of that. Once you've established that, you need to find your fit. Ideally, that will be with an organisation that values individuality over cookie-cutter clones, a place that encourages challenge and embraces different perspectives.

Although there has been a lot of positive progress around the overall diversity, equity and inclusion agenda, organisations still find it hard to culturally change, and it is certainly not something that can be achieved quickly. I've worked with organisations full of round-shaped people in round-shaped holes, who have realised that they need some diversity, some different thinking, so they've said to themselves, for example, 'We want more innovative people.' (Or customer-focused or whatever.) They recruit some square-shaped people, then the existing culture, norms and structures in their organisation are so strong and so deeply embedded that they spend the next few months smoothing down the corners of the square-shaped people, until they are round-shaped and fit into the round holes like everyone else – or they leave, realising they don't fit in. It seems nonsensical, but it happens.

It's not easy for the individuals either. If you don't want to leave or to become round-shaped like everyone else, you need to be brave enough to be yourself and to smash through limiting beliefs (your own and other people's). For that, you need to find who you are and where you fit.

Find who you are

'Bring your whole self to work', 'be your best self', 'be amazing you' – there's plenty of rhetoric around this topic. Mike Robbins has written a whole book about it and Sheryl Sandberg has said, 'I don't believe we have a professional self from Monday through Friday and a real self the rest of the time. It is all professional and it is all personal.' But others, notably, Pilita Clark of the *Financial Times*, implore you *not* to bring your whole self to work, saying that it is absurd to encourage people to behave in the office just as they do at home.

As ever, the truth is somewhere in between these two extremes and the best approach is to apply your common sense. What most people probably want is to be able to be their best at work and at home, and the more these two personas overlap, particularly from a values point of view, the easier it will be.

Speaking of values, it is worth defining your own core values. Like company values, these can seem a bit 'motherhood and apple pie', by which I mean, who wouldn't say honesty was a core value? However, if you can identify the five or six things that are really important to you, they will act as a worthwhile guide to both where and how you develop your career. They will show you the way.

There are lots of examples of personal values online – Indeed.com lists over eighty. They suggest that you print them out, then sort them into three categories: very important, important and not important. Then select the top three to six values you deem to be very important. Don't think too critically during this activity. Just go with your instincts and see what you come up with.

Don't forget, identifying your values and defining what you really believe in is only the start. The next, most important part is what you do, the actions you take (or choose not to take) in line with your values. Just like company values, you want your personal values to be more than just words. Ideally, people who are close to you, at work or at home, should be able to say what your values are from observing your behaviours.

When setting out on your journey of self-discovery, it also helps to know where you're starting from and to have a vision of what good looks like. For that, I'd recommend the 'People Person's Way'. This is a philosophy and a methodology devised by Lara Cullen, which helps you bring out the best in yourself and others by focusing on three core ways to be:

- Be Kind

- Be Brave

- Be Brilliant

Cullen believes that if you adopt these core behaviours for yourself, those around you and your work environment, 'you will be better able to do your best work, be your best self and, little by little, make the world a better place'.

Her three ways of being in the 'People Person's Way' are supported by twelve individual pathways all underpinned by awareness. The visual map of these ways and pathways is represented by her BRing model.

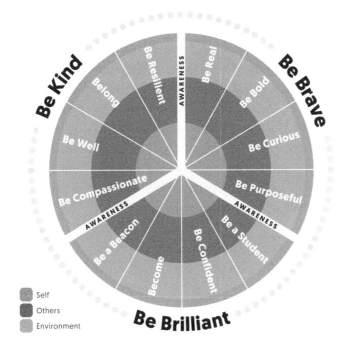

The BRing model

Find where you fit

Once you've got a better idea of who you are, what your values are and what sort of people person you are or want to be, you'll be much better placed to know where you fit. This knowledge could point you towards, or rule out, a particular sector, such as pharma or utilities, or a particular scale of business, such as a start-up or an established plc. Or it could just lead you to seek out your tribe of like-minded people, wherever they work.

Whatever your values, your ideal job should provide you with clear line of sight to the organisation's purpose and to your own personal meaning. According to Gallagher's 2021 *State of the Sector* report, engaging employees around their organisation's purpose, strategy and values is the number one priority for HR and communication professionals. This is because purposeful organisations who share the 'why' have been proven to help reduce employee stress and increase productivity in the workplace.

So, what is a purposeful organisation? Corporate Rebels founder Pim de Morree has defined their common traits as:

- Having a bold purpose that employees can rally around (the why)

- Translating that purpose to everyone in the company – giving clear line of sight

- Hiring for culture and training for skills

- Measuring impact, tracking progress and sharing it widely

- Putting their money where mouth is and really walking the talk

But beware, make sure the organisation you're working with or intending to join lives up to its brand promise. It used to be that a company brand was what was on its product packaging or on the signage on the outside of the building, but these days it's much more about what goes on *inside* the building. Luckily, now it's much easier to see the reality behind the façade, with organisations like Glassdoor.co.uk claiming they can give you the inside scoop on employers big and small. This combined with an unprecedented rise in workplace activism means that, as Sheila Parry advises, organisations need to make sure 'the inner truth of their organisation is as good as its outer promise'.

This level of integrity is one of the key motivators outlined in Parry's PRIDE model – Purpose, Reputation, Integrity, Direction and Energy. It's not surprising that internal communication plays a major role in shaping, delivering and reinforcing all these aspects of an organisation's culture – and it's part of your role to make sure that the messages you are sharing match the reality you are experiencing. If they don't, you'll need to speak truth to power, and that is easier said than done. According to Megan Reitz and John

Higgins in their *Harvard Business Review* article, 'The problem with saying "My door is always open"', the fact that leaders say they have an open-door policy or that they want to be challenged is simplistic. They cite Sam Goldwyn, the American film producer, who said, 'I don't want any yes-men around me. I want everybody to tell me the truth even if it costs them their job.'

A key factor affecting your confidence in speaking out or challenging your leaders is the level of psychological safety you feel. According to Harvard Business School professor Amy Edmondson, who originally came up with the term, 'psychological safety' is a belief that one will not be punished or humiliated for speaking up with ideas, questions, concerns or mistakes.

Only you can decide how safe you feel and which battles to fight, but if it comes to the point where you feel your personal values are challenged, it's probably time to move on. It is not the role of the internal communicator to be a 'spin doctor'. As former Pentagon spokeswoman Torie Clarke says, with apologies to our porcine friends, 'You can put a lot of lipstick on a pig, but it's still a pig.'

 ## Some of my life lessons

I was asked to share some key lessons from life and work with IoIC *Voice* magazine for their 'Voice Over'

column. Here are some extracts from what they published in January 2018.

From an early age, my parents encouraged me to say yes to everything. They didn't, of course, want me to take unnecessary risks, but they did want me to seize every opportunity that came my way. I still err on the side of saying yes to things. This makes for a very full life, which can be tiring, but has resulted in meeting fabulous people and having lots of great experiences over the years.

Takeaway: Say yes more than no.

The flip side of saying yes to everything is never taking no for an answer. When the ironically named 'Success' Comprehensive School told my twin brother and me that they didn't have any UCAS forms because 'no one from this school ever goes to university', we were determined to prove them wrong. We sent off for our own forms and applied to universities ourselves. We got into Birmingham (him) and Aston (me). At Aston, I not only got a degree in business administration, which set me on track for a career in communication, I also met my husband and made some friends for life.

Takeaway: Don't take no for an answer.

As director of communication for a major brewing company, I spent a lot of my time outnumbered by men. This gave me plenty of opportunity to see things from a male point of view. This is really useful as, even today, I can be advising organisations where the majority of employees are men. It's so important to put yourself in the shoes of your audience. Be wary of looking at things through a head-office filter and make sure that what you assume will land with your audience really will be received, understood and acted on. Any decent communication strategy will start with A for audience and that audience will not be made up entirely of people who are just like you. Tailor your communication to those who will be on the receiving end.

Takeaway: One size does not fit all.

It's often said that we have one mouth and two ears and should use them in that proportion – we should listen more than we talk. The temptation as communication professionals is to be in broadcast mode, telling people about our experiences and ideas. But before diving in with solutions, it is important to define the desired outcome. Always ask first: what is it you want your audience to do, say, think and feel differently as an outcome of your communication? Only once the answer to that question is understood can recommendations for effective, sustainable ways to achieve your communication objectives be made and success be measured.

Takeaway: Listen before you leap.

Summary

When delivering internal communication or change programmes, it's not just about what you do, it's also important how you do it. The same applies in our everyday roles – and to fast-track your career, you need to think about both the what and the how.

Using your experience, knowing and applying the right models at the right time, having great technical skills, demonstrating your internal communication superpowers – these are all the foundations on which your career is built. You can't progress far without them, and if you did, you would be on very shaky ground.

But once you have figured out who you are, you will be able to focus on how you do things. You'll know what really matters to you and will be learning, applying and passing on your own life lessons, not just when it comes to technical skills, but also in the way you treat yourself and others. If you find your fit and are lucky enough to work in an organisation whose purpose and values align with your own, then you can be your best and most authentic self, achieving more and leading a happier, healthier life.

Now for my final words of advice: don't get too comfy. Remember, if you are bold you might fail. If you are not bold, you will fail.

Musing 11: OMD – don't worry about others, be the best you can be

Orchestral Manoeuvres in the Dark (OMD) emerged from the Liverpool scene in the late 1970s, but they weren't as cool as Echo and the Bunnymen or Teardrop Explodes. They were signed to Factory Records, but weren't as cult as Joy Division, New Order or Happy Mondays. They pioneered synth pop, but weren't as recognised for doing so as Kraftwerk or Gary Numan.

But here's the thing: OMD realised they had no control over what these other bands were doing. Instead, they focused on doing their own thing. They wrote hit songs, played great gigs (I went to a couple), built a loyal fan base and featured on the soundtracks of cult movies like *Pretty in Pink*.

Forty years on and they've sold over 40 million records. And, watching the footage of their 2019 Hammersmith Apollo performance, they look like they're still enjoying themselves.

So, what can we learn from OMD? Don't get distracted by what or how well you think others are doing. Focus all your energy on being the best that you can be.

Conclusion

Ultimately, it's the leaders and line managers in your organisation who are responsible for engaging and communicating with their teams. But just as they turn to experts in marketing, finance and IT for specialist help and support, so they will seek out expert internal communicators to provide them with the advice, tools and techniques they need to do this effectively.

As the people within organisations are increasingly being recognised as the only real source of competitive advantage, then your role takes on even more importance. Now is the time to take your seat at the top table, to become a trusted advisor and to add real value by being more strategic and, most of all, by being you.

Use Part One of this book to demonstrate the value of internal communication, to prove to those around you that, done correctly, it will build trust within your organisation and have a significant impact on employee engagement, culture and productivity.

Use Part Two, and especially the ABCDE model, to make sure you are taking a strategic and professional approach. That applies first to identifying what the real problem or opportunity is and then to coming up with internal communication solutions that will work to address them.

Use Part Three to fast-track your career. It's one thing to know how to be strategic, it's another to actually do it. Be clear about your purpose, plan well, spend your time wisely and learn how to say no. The more you do those things, the more value you will add and the more options will open up for you.

Don't wait for this to happen – take control of your career. Be proactive. Decide your next move or your ultimate dream job, identify what you need to get there, and take the steps to make it happen. Learn skills, get experience, build networks, share best practice. Along the way, I guarantee you'll meet some great people and have some epic adventures.

I wish you every success. I hope your internal communication career makes you fulfilled, happy and proud.

If you'd like any further advice, or just want to share your story, then please get in touch. Contact details are on The Author page at the end of the book.

References

Introduction

M Stephens/Guitar.com (2017) 'Duane Allman: The guitar legend's life in music', Guitar.com, https://guitar.com/features/duane-allman, accessed 27 August 2021

Chapter 1

Michael Chui et al (2012) 'The social economy: Unlocking value and productivity through social technologies', McKinsey Global Institute, www.mckinsey.com/industries/technology-media-and-telecommunications/our-insights/the-social-economy, accessed 31 July 2021

Corporate Leadership Council (2004) *Driving Performance and Retention Through Employee Engagement*, Corporate Executive Board, https://stcloudstate.edu/humanresources/_files/documents/supv-brown-bag/employee-engagement.pdf, accessed 31 July 2021

TE Deal and AA Kennedy (1982) *Corporate Cultures: The rites and rituals of corporate life*, Addison-Wesley

Gallup (2018) *Gallup's Approach to Culture: Building a culture that drives performance*, Gallup, https://gallup.com/workplace/232682/culture-paper-2018.aspx, accessed 31 July 2021

David MacLeod and Nita Clarke (2009) *Engaging for Success: Enhancing performance through employee engagement*, Department for Business, Innovation and Skills, https://engageforsuccess.org/wp-content/uploads/2021/02/Engaging-for-Success.pdf, accessed 31 July 2021

David MacLeod and Nita Clarke et al (2012) *The Evidence*, Engage for Success, https://engageforsuccess.org/wp-content/uploads/2015/09/The-Evidence.pdf, accessed 31 July 2021

Rebecca Peters (2020) 'Employee communication', CIPD, www.cipd.co.uk/knowledge/fundamentals/

relations / communication / factsheet#gref, accessed
31 July 2021

Tonia E Ries et al (2021) *2021 Edelman Trust Barometer*,
Edelman, www.edelman.com / sites / g / files / aatuss191 /
files / 2021-01 / 2021-edelman-trust-barometer.pdf,
accessed 31 July 2021

Chapter 2

George Goodall (2015) 'What is the history of
the RACI chart?', Facetation, http:/ / facetation.
blogspot.ch / 2015 / 05 / what-is-history-of-raci-chart.
html, accessed 31 July 2021

Francis Gouillart and Frederick D Sturdivant (Jan–
Feb 1994) 'Spend a day in the life of your customers',
Harvard Business Review, https:/ / hbr.org / 1994 / 01 /
spend-a-day-in-the-life-of-your-customers, accessed
31 July 2021

Travis M Hessman (2013) 'Today's consumers
will no longer accept one-size-fits-all. Nor do they
expect it', *Industry Week*, www.industryweek.com /
innovation / article / 21960676 / innovation-one-size-
fits-one, accessed 31 July 2021

James Timpson (2021) 'Yes! It's time to escape the
"sales-prevention" office', *The Sunday Times*, www.
thetimes.co.uk / article / yes-its-time-to-escape-the-

sales-prevention-office-jf92h3kkc, accessed 31 July 2021

Ciaran Varley (2020) 'Marcus Rashford: Feeding Britain's children – inside his campaign to tackle child hunger', BBC Sport, www.bbc.co.uk/sport/football/55338104, accessed 31 July 2021

Chapter 3

CIPD (2021) 'Employee engagement: An evidence review', CIPD, www.cipd.co.uk/knowledge/fundamentals/relations/engagement/evidence-engagement, accessed 31 July 2021

George Doran (1981) 'There's a S.M.A.R.T. way to write management's goals and objectives', *Management Review*, 70, 35–36, https://community.mis.temple.edu/mis0855002fall2015/files/2015/10/S.M.A.R.T-Way-Management-Review.pdf, accessed 31 July 2021

Institute of Internal Communication (no date) 'Our purpose', Institute of Internal Communication, www.ioic.org.uk/wematteratwork/our-purpose, accessed 31 July 2021

Daniel H Pink (2010) *Drive: The surprising truth about what motivates us*, Canongate Books

BF Skinner (1965) *Science and Human Behavior*, Simon & Schuster

Chapter 4

Steve and Cindy Crescenzo (2020) 'Cutting through the clutter: Creating comms that people will actually pay attention to and act on' (*Voices* webinar), Staffbase, https://youtu.be/BLjy1rv1KFg, accessed 31 July 2021

The Community Roundtable (2021) 'Community manager advancement day', The Community Roundtable, https://communityroundtable.com/community-manager-advancement-day-cmad-2021, accessed 31 July 2021

Alyson Gausby et al (2015) *Attention Spans*, Consumer Insights, Microsoft Canada, http://dl.motamem.org/microsoft-attention-spans-research-report.pdf, accessed 31 July 2021

William Penn (no date) 'Of conduct in speech' in *Fruits of Solitude* in *The Harvard Classics Vol 1 Part 3* (1909–1914) PF Collier & Son (2001), Bartleby.com, https://bartleby.com/1/3/209.html, accessed 31 July 2021

Herbert Simon (1978) cited in Alyson Gausby et al (2015) *Attention Spans*, Consumer Insights, Microsoft

Canada, http://dl.motamem.org/microsoft-attention-spans-research-report.pdf, accessed 31 July 2021

Chapter 5

Andy Barrow and Frazer Rendell (2020) speaking at 'Engage to perform – learn from elite athletes how to create high-performing teams', Engage for Success, 10 July 2020

David Bradford and Carole Robin (2021) *Connect: Building exceptional relationships with family, friends and colleagues*, Penguin

ClearBox Consulting (2021) *Employee Apps Report V1.1*, ClearBox Consulting, www.clearbox.co.uk/employee-apps-report

Local Government Association (no date) 'Communicating with your line managers', Local Government Association, www.local.gov.uk/communicating-your-line-managers, accessed 31 July 2021

Melcrum (2013) *Innovation and Intervention in Manager Communication* and *Towers Watson Change and Communication ROI* both quoted in *Engage for Success* (no date) 'Show 46: Innovation and intervention in manager communication' with Bec Richmond, https://engageforsuccess.org/engage-for-success-radio-podcast/show-46-innovation-and-intervention-in-manager-communication, accessed 31 July 2021

MetLife (2021) *United Kingdom Employee Benefit Trends Study*, MetLife, www.metlife.co.uk/content/dam/metlifecom/uk/pdf/EmployeeBenefits/Brexit/1/1751.04MAR2021-EBTS-STUDY_WEB.pdf, accessed 31 July 2021

Rachel Miller (2016) 'Ten new trends in communication', All Things IC, www.allthingsic.com/trendsintranet, accessed 31 July 2021

Pull no Punches (2020) 'Pull No Punches (Season 1) with Bill Quirke', Masgroves, https://pullnopunches.podbean.com/e/pull-no-punches-with-bill-quirke, accessed 31 July 2021

John Smythe (2007) *The CEO: Chief Engagement Officer: Turning hierarchy upside down to drive performance*, Gower

Minna Wang (2020) 'Leadership: What are the characteristics of a great leader?', Smarp, https://blog.smarp.com/leadership-what-are-the-qualities-and-characteristics-of-a-great-leader, accessed 31 July 2021

Chapter 6

Acas (no date) 'Informing and consulting your employees about workplace matters', Acas, www. acas.org.uk/informing-and-consulting-with-your-employees-about-workplace-matters, accessed 31 July 2021

William Bruce Cameron (1963) *Informal Sociology: A casual introduction to sociological thinking*, Random House

Michele E Ewing (2018) '22 standards to measure and shape internal communications' in *Strategies & Tactics*, PRSA, https://apps.prsa.org/ StrategiesTactics/Articles/view/12218/1156/22_ Standards_to_Measure_and_Shape_Internal_ Communi#.YMXzu_lKg2w, accessed 31 July 2021

Gatehouse (2019) *State of the Sector: The definitive global survey of the internal communication profession*, Gatehouse

Trudi Lewis, Jenni Field et al (2019) *Research Report 2019: Measurement and ROI for internal communication*, CIPR in association with IoIC, www.ioic.org.uk/ files/2133_CIPR_IoIC_Research_Report_2019.pdf, accessed 31 July 2021

Rachel Miller (2014) 'How to carry out internal communication audits', All Things IC, www. allthingsic.com/audit, accessed 31 July 2021

J O'Neil et al/Institute for Public Relations (2018)
A Delphi Study to Identify Standards for Internal
Communication, *Public Relations Journal*, Vol 11 Issue
3, https://prjournal.instituteforpr.org/wp-content/
uploads/1.-A-Delphi-Study-to-Identify-Standards-
for-IC-1-1.pdf

Bill Quirke (2008) *Making the Connections: Using
internal communication to turn strategy into action* (2nd
edn), Routledge

Survey Monkey (no date) 'Survey sample size',
Survey Monkey, www.surveymonkey.com/mp/
sample-size, accessed 31 July 2021

Chapter 7

Chris Bevolo (2010) *A Marketer's Guide to Measuring
Results: Prove the impact of new media and traditional
healthcare marketing efforts*, HCPro

Rob Davies (2021) 'Brewdog co-founder apologises
to ex-staff over "toxic" working environment', *The
Guardian*, www.theguardian.com/business/2021/
jun/11/brewdog-co-founder-apologises-to-ex-staff-
over-toxic-working-environment, accessed 1 August
2021

Margaret Heffernan and Helen Lewis (2020) *The
Spark*, BBC Radio 4, www.bbc.co.uk/programmes/
m000gsm8, accessed 1 August 2021

Interact Software (2018) *Communicating in Crisis*, Interact Software, www.interactsoftware.com/wp-content/uploads/2018/07/Communicating-in-Crisis-Interact-Software-1-1.pdf, accessed 1 August 2021

Bill McFarlan (2003) *Drop the Pink Elephant*, Capstone

Chapter 8

Zora Artis et al (2020) 'Think differently: How to ensure your employee communications drive business outcomes' (webinar), Poppulo, www.poppulo.com/resources/think-differently-how-to-ensure-your-employee-communications-drive-business-outcomes, accessed 1 August 2021

Steve and Cindy Crescenzo (2020) 'Cutting through the clutter: Creating comms that people will actually pay attention to and act on' (*Voices* webinar), Staffbase, https://youtu.be/BLjy1rv1KFg, accessed 31 July 2021

Kate Jones (6 November 2020) *Values in a Covid Climate*, Virtual Employee Engagement Summit, Engage Business Media

Elletra Scrivo (2020) 'Leaving lockdown – internal comms and the new normal', *Communicate Magazine*, www.communicatemagazine.com/news/2020/leaving-lockdown-internal-comms-and-the-new-normal, accessed 1 August 2021

Richard Wiseman (2008) 'New Year's resolution project', Quirkology, www.richardwiseman.com/ quirkology/new/USA/Experiment_resolution. shtml, accessed 1 August 2021

Chapter 9

Nick Cave (no date) *The Red Hand Files*, The Red Hand Files, www.theredhandfiles.com, accessed 1 August 2021

Chapter 10

Lesley Allman (2020) '10 things you need to get right when launching a new business', re:find, https:// refind.co.uk/launching-a-new-business, accessed 1 August 2021

Anthony Burrill (2017) *Make It Now!*, Penguin Random House

CIPR (2021) 'Learn & develop', CIPR, https://cipr. co.uk/CIPR/Learn_and_develop/CIPR/Learn_ and_develop_.aspx?hkey=0f864aa6-6437-4175-9667-ed3ede055a77, accessed 1 August 2021

International Association of Business Communicators (IABC) Academy, www.iabc.com/Learn/ IABC-Academy

IoIC (2021) 'IoIC Profession Map', The Institute
of Internal Communication, https://ioic.org.uk/
professional-development/ioic-profession-map-2,
accessed 1 August 2021

Plato, www.goodreads.com/quotes/506943-wise-
men-talk-because-they-have-something-to-say-fools

PR Academy (2021) 'Internal Communication', PR
Academy, https://pracademy.co.uk/courses/category/
internal-communication, accessed 1 August 2021

Smarp (2020) *The Great Comms Debate 5*, Smarp,
https://resources.smarp.com/the-great-comms-
debate-5, accessed 1 August 2021

Eleanor Tweddell (2020) *Why Losing Your Job Could Be
the Best Thing That Ever Happened to You: Five simple
steps to thrive after redundancy*, Penguin Business

VMA Group (2021) *The Communications Function:
Taking the temperature*, VMA Group, www.vmagroup.
com/taking-the-temperature-survey, accessed 1
August 2021

Chapter 11

Lesley Allman (2018) 'Don't speak up if you've
got nothing to say', Voice, The Institute of Internal
Communication, https://voice.ioic.org.uk/item/644-

don-t-speak-up-if-you-ve-got-nothing-to-say, accessed
1 August 2021

Pilita Clark (2015) 'Please do not bring your
"whole self" to work', *Financial Times,* www.
ft.com/content/595d035a-ee72-11e8-8180-
9cf212677a57, accessed 1 August 2021

Torie Clarke (2006) *Lipstick on a Pig: Winning in the no-
spin era by someone who knows the game,* Free Press

Lara Cullen (2021) *How to Be a People Person: Be kind.
Be brave. Be brilliant,* SRA Books

Pim de Morree (2020) speaking at 'Beyond crisis: How
to engage your people in turbulent times' (bootcamp),
Poppulo, https://poppulo.com/blog/this-is-
unmissable-an-amazing-line-up-and-no-travel-no-cost-
poppulo-s-virtual-bootcamp, accessed 1 August 2021

Amy Edmondson (2018) *The Fearless Organization:
Creating psychological safety in the workplace for
learning, innovation, and growth,* Wiley

Gallagher (2021) *State of the Sector 2021: Global
internal communication and employee engagement trends,*
Gallagher, www.ajg.com/employeeexperience/state-
of-the-sector-2021, accessed 1 August 2021

Herbert Smith Freehills (2019) *Future of Work:
Adapting to the democratised workplace,* Herbert

Smith Freehills, www.herbertsmithfreehills.com/latest-thinking/the-new-world-of-work-report-warns-of-an-unprecedented-rise-in-workplace-activism-v2, accessed 1 August 2021

Sheila Parry (2018) *Take Pride: How to build organisational success through your people*, Unbound

Megan Reitz and John Higgins (2017) 'The problem with saying "My door is always open"', *Harvard Business Review*, https://hbr.org/2017/03/the-problem-with-saying-my-door-is-always-open#comment-section, accessed 1 August 2021

Mike Robbins (2018) *Bring Your Whole Self to Work: How vulnerability unlocks creativity, connection, and performance*, Hay House Business

Sheryl Sandberg (2013) *Lean In: Women, work, and the will to lead*, WH Allen

Acknowledgements

I guess I've got the coronavirus pandemic of 2020 to thank for writing this book. For the first time in my career, I had a bit of a lull and that gave me time for two of life's luxuries: thinking and learning.

My thinking was vastly improved by the fabulous structure and inspiration provided by Eleanor Tweddell and Amanda Parradine at Another Door. My learning was fuelled by the amazing array of internal communication specialists and other thought leaders who shared their expertise online during lockdown. I usually have to leave my Derbyshire village to seek inspiration, diversity of thought and innovative ideas, but the unique circumstances meant I had virtual access to all of this and more. Many of the inspiring people I met and things I learnt have made their way into this book.

Having decided to write a book, but knowing nothing about how to go about it, I was grateful for the advice of some people who had already done so. Thanks to Sheila Parry, Eleanor Tweddell, Lara Cullen and Elaine Penhaul, who gave me valuable pointers that led me to take the plunge and find a publisher. Booksmith Joe Laredo helped me to organise my thoughts into a structure that could become a book and the team at Rethink Press have subsequently guided me through the publishing process. I'm also very grateful to my beta readers, Karen McElroy and Caroline Redhead, who reviewed my early drafts and provided considered, thorough and much-valued feedback. Finally, I'm indebted to Rachel Miller for reading my manuscript and providing wise counsel, as well as for her lovely foreword.

Of course, there were long periods of just bashing out words on my PC, but I thoroughly enjoyed the process of putting what was in my head onto paper and supplementing it with new discoveries along the way. But there wouldn't actually have been anything in my head to share if it had not been for the many colleagues, suppliers and clients that I have worked with over the twenty years I've been specialising in internal communication. The individuals are too numerous to mention, but you know who you are. I've listed below more than fifty organisations I have provided internal communication support to during that time. I'm grateful to all of them for entrusting their internal communication and employee engagement to me, and for everything I have learnt from them along the way.

I feel privileged to have spent my working life doing something I love and that I believe benefits lots of other people, helping them to love their working lives too.

I hope that you benefit from me passing on some of my learnings, that you enjoy putting them into practice and that they help you to make a positive contribution to the incredible world of internal communication.

Organisations I have supported:

- Acteon Group
- Advance Housing and Support
- Aggregate Industries
- Alliance Healthcare
- Alstom
- Avis
- Aviva (via McCann)
- Baxter Neumann
- Boots
- Britvic
- Burton Biscuits
- C&C Group (Magners)
- Capgemini
- Carlsberg UK
- Carphone Warehouse
- CE Electric
- Centrica Storage
- Domestic & General

- DS Smith
- Energizer
- Enterprise Inns
- ESAB Holdings
- Evergreen Garden Care
- Gilead Sciences
- GXO
- Halfords
- Healthcare Initial
- Hovis
- Interserve
- Jeakins Weir
- Kuehne+Nagel
- Leidos
- Lloyds Banking Group
- Marks & Spencer
- Mitchells & Butlers
- Molson Coors
- National Grid (via McCann)
- Network Rail
- No7 Beauty Company
- Pattonair
- PepsiCo UK & Ireland
- Portman Group
- Premier Foods
- Pukka Pies
- PwC
- Quorn
- Royal Horticultural Society
- Screwfix
- Serco
- SHS Condiments & Sauces
- St Andrew's Healthcare
- Standard Brands
- Wattbike
- WBA Global Sourcing
- XPO Logistics

The Author

Lesley has over twenty years of internal communication and employee engagement experience.

Most recently, she has headed up Allman Communication, supporting leadership teams in over fifty leading organisations and successfully helping them to deliver major transformation and culture change programmes.

Prior to that, she led in-house communication teams at Coors Brewers and Premier Foods, where, after the acquisition of Campbell's and RHM, internal communication played a key role in engaging and aligning the organisation behind a new purpose, vision, strategy and values.

She is a Fellow of the Institute of Internal Communication and her work has won numerous industry awards including IoIC, FEIEA, CIPR, CorpComms and, in 2020, Communicate Magazine's Internal Communication & Engagement Gold Award for her work with Carlsberg UK.

⊕ www.allmancommunication.co.uk

in www.linkedin.com/in/allmancommunication

🐦 @allmancomms

lesley@allmancommunication.com

Made in the USA
Las Vegas, NV
29 November 2022

60594146R00138